Media Audiences

Key Concerns in Media Studies

Series editor: Andrew Crisell

Within the context of today's global, digital environment, *Key Concerns in Media Studies* addresses themes and concepts that are integral to the study of media. Concisely written by leading academics, the books consider the historical development of these themes and the theories that underpin them, and assess their overall significance, using up-to-date examples and case studies throughout. By giving a clear overview of each topic, the series provides an ideal starting point for all students of modern media.

Published

Paul Bowman   *Culture and the Media*
Andrew Crisell   *Liveness and Recording in the Media*
Stuart Cunningham, Terry Flew and Adam Swift   *Media Economics*
Tim Dwyer   *Legal and Ethical Issues in the Media*
Katie Ellis and Gerard Goggin   *Disability and the Media*
Gerard Goggin   *New Technologies and the Media*
David Hendy   *Public Service Broadcasting*
Monika Metykova   *Diversity and the Media*
Shaun Moores   *Media, Place and Mobility*
Sarah Niblock   *Media Professionalism and Training*
Sean Redmond   *Celebrity and the Media*
Niall Richardson and Sadie Wearing   *Gender in the Media*
Sue Turnbull   *Media Audiences*

Media Audiences

Is Anybody Watching?

Sue Turnbull

© Sue Turnbull, under exclusive licence to Macmillan Education Limited 2020

All rights reserved. No reproduction, copy or transmission of this publication may be made without written permission.

No portion of this publication may be reproduced, copied or transmitted save with written permission or in accordance with the provisions of the Copyright, Designs and Patents Act 1988, or under the terms of any licence permitting limited copying issued by the Copyright Licensing Agency, Saffron House, 6–10 Kirby Street, London EC1N 8TS.

Any person who does any unauthorized act in relation to this publication may be liable to criminal prosecution and civil claims for damages.

The author has asserted her right to be identified as the author of this work in accordance with the Copyright, Designs and Patents Act 1988.

First published 2020 by
RED GLOBE PRESS

Red Globe Press in the UK is an imprint of Macmillan Education Limited, registered in England, company number 01755588, of 4 Crinan Street, London, N1 9XW.

Red Globe Press® is a registered trademark in the United States, the United Kingdom, Europe and other countries.

ISBN 978-1-352-00958-3 hardback
ISBN 978-1-137-40510-4 paperback

This book is printed on paper suitable for recycling and made from fully managed and sustained forest sources. Logging, pulping and manufacturing processes are expected to conform to the environmental regulations of the country of origin.

A catalogue record for this book is available from the British Library.

A catalog record for this book is available from the Library of Congress.

Contents

List of Illustrations and Figure vii
Acknowledgements ix

1 Introductions 1
2 What is a Media Audience? 21
3 Technologies of Audiencing 39
4 Content and Interpretation 61
5 The People who Matter 85
6 The Madness in our Method 109

Reference List 129

Index 139

List of Illustrations and Figure

Illustrations

2.1 Family viewing – although in this image the TV has yet to be switched on — 22
2.2 A cinema audience in waiting — 22
2.3 How people used to read the news on the train — 23
2.4 Family viewing in the internet connected home — 23
2.5 Audiencing on a train? — 24
3.1 An illuminated page from the Gospel of St Matthew from *the Book of Kells* — 41
4.1 A lonely tree in Iceland — 65
4.2 Cover illustration, Barry Blitt, The New Yorker, February 1, 2016. © Condé Nast — 72

Figure

2.1 The dimensions of audiencing — 29

Acknowledgements

This book has been a long time in the making. For their patience and encouragement, I'd like to thank series editor, Andrew Crisell, and all the Palgrave Macmillan and Red Globe Press staff who have provided their assistance over the intervening years. For introducing me to the field of audience research, I'd like to thank Peter B. White for his timely introduction to the remarkable TV series *Prisoner Cell Block H* and its teen audiences in 1984. I'd also like to thank Robyn Penman for her guidance and insistence on the importance of communication in the formation of our social experiences of the world. My colleagues and students at the University of Wollongong continue to sustain me with their good humour, invaluable insights and their ongoing interest in this project. Particular thanks are due to Kate Bowles, Renee Middlemost, Chris Moore and Ika Willis, the tireless cheer squad every academic needs, and Kai Soh for much needed last minute assistance. Last but by no means least, thanks to my family, Will and Rick, for everything else.

1 Introductions

It's 1987 and I'm on my way from one side (the outer east) of Melbourne's vast suburban sprawl, to the other (the inner west), to undertake a year-long study of the role of the media in the lives of a group of young women in a girls' secondary school. I've not long been in Australia (three years), and am only just beginning to get a handle on its troubled settler–colonial history and social complexities. As will become apparent, the 50-minute car drive (on a good day) that transports me from my home in a leafy suburb populated by middle-class Anglo-Australians and migrants from northern Europe, who arrived *before* the Second World War, to the state-funded high school in a working-class inner-city suburb that has witnessed waves of *post-war* migration, is about to present me with a whole set of new challenges in thinking about Australia, people and the media in their lives.

This is the formative experience that will underpin my approach to audience research over the next 30 years as the media landscape has gradually evolved, and I am returning to this experience because, after accepting the challenge of writing a book about audiences in a series entitled 'Key Concerns in Media Studies', when it came to the point of defining just what those current concerns might be, I hesitated. While I have been encouraging undergraduate and postgraduate students to embrace audience research for the last 30 years, when faced with trying to define the field, and how best to proceed, I needed some time to think this through. In a globalized, fragmented, converged digital media environment, is the concept of the media audience still viable, I wondered. As I hope this book will demonstrate, I think it is, but we can learn much from the past of media audience research in seeking to move forward. Inspired by the French axiom 'Reculer pour mieux sauter', which might be roughly translated as the value of retreating a few steps in order to make a better leap forward, I decided to return to the history of media audience research first. I wanted to explore once again the why, when, where and how of this complex field as it has developed over the years in order to suggest how we might proceed. What can we learn from this history that will help us understand how audiences manage the complex media environment in which they are embedded today? As will become evident, while audiences have always been 'active' in their use of the media, every new media technology or form is almost always framed in terms of the imagined 'effects' that it will have on the audience that consumes it.

The backstory

While an interest in media audiences arguably begins with the emergence of the steam-driven printing press media in the 19th century, my own interest in the field began in a very different time and place. As a teacher of English working in a secondary school outside Cambridge in the UK in the mid-1970s, I discovered that talking about the media with a group of students who were classified as 'disadvantaged' was a way to get them to discuss, and even tentatively write about, films and TV shows which they had enjoyed. Some of these students came from tiny rural hamlets and had never been to Cambridge despite the fact they lived only 10 miles from the city centre. This was the class of 'no-hopers' to whom, as a newly minted eager young teacher, I was supposed to give some cheer, and perhaps even some literacy skills. As I discovered, these students were avid consumers of the media in the form of what has now come to be called 'the legacy media'. This included television, radio, comics and magazines. Furthermore, they were well able to express their opinions and argue the case for the content they liked or disliked, even if we started from the position 'It's rubbish, Miss.' For a teacher of English desperate to get students to extend their skills in reading and writing by whatever means, inviting students to think, talk and write about the media they encountered became a means to an end, one that had been advocated during my teacher training experience.

While undertaking a Postgraduate Certificate in Education in the Department of Education in Cambridge in the early 1970s, we were introduced to the work of the Education Unit of the British Film Institute. This included the materials available for film study in schools which came in 'packages' that included 16 mm film clips and study guides organized around such topics as 'The Hollywood Blonde', 'The Western' and 'Horror'. While these topics were more indicative of the concerns of the burgeoning field of cinema studies than they were the interests of the students with whom I was working, my pupils nonetheless welcomed the weekly screenings. Showing the reels of film clips that arrived by post every week was not, however, easy. This endeavour demanded both commitment and a bit of muscle since it involved lugging a heavy Bell and Howell 16 mm film projector, and a cumbersome screen, into remote classrooms that were rarely equipped with any form of blackout. But the enjoyment of the clips, the lively discussions that ensued and the sheer potential of film studies in the classroom impressed me from the first. Teaching about television, it should be noted, was more of a challenge since we were unable to bring the object of study into the classroom except in the form of TV guides. Within a decade the introduction of the video recorder connected to a TV monitor on a stand equipped with wheels would make both film and television studies much easier, although the small screen was frustrating. However, during the 1970s teaching about any form of media other than film or radio was largely restricted to analysing and critiquing printed materials, such as the news in newspapers and advertising in magazines.

Despite these limitations, it was this experience of teaching media that inspired me to return to university in 1984 to undertake a doctoral degree in media education at La Trobe University in Melbourne. While cinema studies had recently found its niche in the undergraduate curriculum, media studies was taught only in the Graduate School of Education where the primary purpose was to teach teachers how to teach students to think critically about the popular media in order to resist its presumably pernicious effects. This was the gate-keeping function for media studies pre-figured in 1933 by Frank Leavis and Denys Thompson in their highly influential book *Culture and Environment: The Training of Critical Awareness*. Here Leavis and Thompson set the agenda for a 'prophylactic approach' to teaching about the media and popular culture, the goal being to teach students to discount media messages so that they might not be impregnated by the 'crude emotional falsity' and 'illusory values' of popular culture (Buckingham, 1993, p. 214). The possibility that the popular culture they encountered in the media might have some intrinsic value was simply unthinkable. It was therefore implicit that those wanting to teach about the media in schools were not supposed to like the object of their study, but to hold the media in healthy disdain because of its presumed negative effects on society. It was this assumption of negative effects that was one of the key reasons I wanted to undertake audience research, since my experience with the students I had been teaching in England had led me to question this routine dismissal of the popular.

In Australia in the early 1980s, as in the UK and the USA, the issues about the media being routinely canvassed in and on the media included both the negative effects of the media in general, and some media in particular. This included representations of violence, but also the representation of gender inspired by a growing wave of feminist critique. Occasionally these concerns coincided, as in the case of the Australian soap opera *Prisoner*, known internationally as *Prisoner: Cell Block H*. With its representation of unglamorous women of all shapes and sizes, as well as its initially tentative approach to the depiction of same-sex relationships, *Prisoner* was simultaneously reviled in the popular press and applauded for its groundbreaking depiction of women (Turnbull, 2017). As Alan McKee (2001) has pointed out, during the 1980s more academic 'ethnographic' work was devoted to *Prisoner* than any other series in the history of Australian television (p. 184). Meanwhile, Australia's other famous export, *Neighbours*, was largely ignored by scholars, though not by the popular media. Indeed, I was invited by the commercial Channel Ten to appear on a nationally broadcast breakfast show direct from the Ramsay Street location of the show as a 'soapologist' (not my chosen title) in order to explain how and why *Neighbours* had come to be on the front cover of *Time* magazine and why British viewers in their millions had embraced an unpretentious Australian suburban soap. There was, however, no audience research available for me at that time to cite, despite increasing academic interest in the popularity of soap operas as a genre.

During the 1980s, soap opera, and other genres favoured by women, became the focus of a number of studies inspired by what has been described as the second wave of feminism (Lotz, 2003). In 1982, Tania Modleski published *Loving with a Vengeance*, a study of gothic romance and soap operas that would herald a wave of feminist audience research in the following decade. Ien Ang would publish, first in the Netherlands (1982), and then in the UK and the USA (1985), her influential study of the Dutch audience for the American prime time melodrama *Dallas*, while Janice Radway (1984) would undertake a ground-breaking study of women romance readers in the American Midwest. As Liesbet van Zoonen (1994, p. 105) suggested, the turn to a focus on media audiences and their reception of these media texts was in part a reaction to the 'textual determinism' implicit in earlier approaches that assumed an effect from an analysis of the content. This was particularly the case in debates about media representation and the perceived need for more positive images of women.

One of the first books of feminist media scholarship I encountered when I arrived in Australia was *Media She* (1974), Patricia Edgar and Hilary McPhee's searing take on the ways in which women were depicted in advertisements of the time. Culminating in a rather twee set of photographs featuring a bearded male in feminized poses to make the point, *Media She* predated Erving Goffman's *Gender Advertisements* (1976) by two years. With a foreword by a key figure in the history of British cultural studies, Richard Hoggart, and a long essay by Goffman (1976), *Gender Advertisements* addressed such topics as 'The Feminine Touch' and 'The Ritualization of Subordination' in order to illustrate how advertising images reinforced women's secondary status in society. The publication of Judith Williamson's *Decoding Advertising: Ideology and Meaning* (1978) subsequently introduced a new level of theoretical complexity by applying a structuralist-semiotic approach to an analysis of advertisements as complex ideological signs. It was as a result of interventions such as these that the representation of women in the media became the ideological battleground that it continues to be today, even though, as Amanda Lotz has pointed out (2003, p. 8), we have now passed through many different waves of feminist critique and activism.

As someone interested in media education, I could see the potential for teaching Williamson's approach in the classroom. However, I wanted to explore just how the popular media might be received and appropriated (to use the language of the day) by 'real people' in the course of their daily lives. In particular, I was interested in the use of the media by the young people with whom I had been working in the UK. I'd read a collection of essays edited by Stuart Hall and Tony Jefferson entitled 'Resistance through Rituals: Youth Subcultures in Post-War Britain' (1975), one of a series of Working Papers in Cultural Studies produced by the recently established Birmingham Centre for Cultural Studies, and I was intrigued by the suggestion that popular culture might be appropriated by students in their resistance to school, as well as other forms of authority. In particular, I was provoked by an essay by Angela McRobbie and Jenny Garber entitled 'Girls and Subcultures' (1975), in which they suggest that the female of the species had largely been ignored in 'youth studies'. As a graduate of what McRobbie and Graber identified as the 'culture of the bedroom' in a depressed post-industrial town in the north of England, I wanted to know more about the role of the media in girls' lives, and how it might shape their view of the world.[1] Or not, as the case

---

[1] I was a member of the Beatles fan club in 1963 and could remember just how important receiving a Christmas message on a flexible vinyl disc was to my 13-year-old self.

might be, since I knew from personal experience that the role of the media in young people's complicated lives was complex.

In thinking about the kind of study I wanted to conduct, I had also been impressed by Paul Willis' *Learning to Labour* (1977), an account of his experience as a teacher in a secondary school in the north of England, an environment with which I also identified. Here Willis explores how the cultures of masculinity operational in the school and the community ensure that working-class 'lads' will continue to get working-class jobs and inevitably be excluded from professional careers and social advancement. Once again, I was more interested in the girls in Willis' story who play only a minor role (as the girlfriend or 'the missus'). I wanted to know how they saw the culture in which they were embedded. What were options for them? And what role did the media play in thinking about their futures? After reading the French Marxist philosopher Louis Althusser's influential but depressing essay 'On Ideology' (1971), I was alert to the ways in which the social formations of the family and the school, in conjunction with the ideological apparatus of the media, might function as forms of state control, limiting the ways in which people might think about themselves and the social structures in which they were located. I was, however, once again somewhat sceptical, based on my own experience of the world. As both a student and teacher, I was idealistic enough to believe in human agency, in the power of education and the media, to inform and to enable people to think differently and to bring about social change.

Back on the road across Melbourne, I'm therefore on a mission. My goal is to spend a year in a secondary school, to select a group of girls with whom I will work closely in order to understand the role of the media in their lives. I want to know what they are watching, what they are reading, what they are listening to and how this complex media landscape relates to how they see themselves and their future. In this endeavour, I am inspired not only by McRobbie, Garber and Willis but also by Hermann Bausinger's call for an understanding of media practices in the conduct of everyday life as outlined in an article translated from the German and published in the academic journal *Media, Culture & Society* in 1984. In this essay, Bausinger describes two days in the life of Mr Meier and his attempts to follow the football while also negotiating his relationship with his wife and son. It's a vivid portrait, revealing the intricacy of family relations and attachments to the media.

In his conclusion, Bausinger makes a number of key points:

- That a meaningful study of a person's use of the media will inevitably involve the media ensemble with which they engage.

- That as a rule, the media are not used completely or with full concentration.
- That the media are an integral part of the ways in which everyday life is conducted.
- That the media are always consumed in a social context.
- And lastly, that media communication cannot be separated from direct personal communication.

While I found this an exciting set of propositions, it is not entirely clear from Bausinger's essay exactly how one might go about conducting such a study. Bausinger has little to say about methodology, except to suggest that forms of empirical research in which qualitative methods, such as participant observation, *introspections* (my italics), depth interviews and case studies might be useful (1984, p. 347). In the end, he concludes, what is needed is a 'bit of wild thinking to catch and describe this complex world in all its rational irrationality' (Bausinger, 1984, p. 351).

As part of that 'wild thinking', I began by conceiving of the 22 girls who would participate in my study first and foremost as people rather than as a specific media audience for a specific media text.[2] While Nick Couldry will later call for a study of the media practices in the context of everyday life (2004) and Shaun Moores (2018) and others have advocated for a non-media centric approach to media research, I'm already there. In order to make sense of how the girls negotiate the media in their lives, I have decided to embrace a notion of the self and the concept of 'a moral career' borrowed from the work of the British sociologist Romano Harré (1979).

In *Social Being*, Harré suggests that all human beings, whatever their different social context, are in a continual process of managing their conduct in relation to the competing moral orders in their lives. Following Harré, I'm convinced that central to human agency is a person's capacity to imagine different courses of action and how these might affect their future, even if such futures may not be acted upon. As Harré, suggests, this is a social theory that sheds light on the dialectic between individual experience and the social formation. The concept of a moral career therefore acknowledges the power of social formations to constrain and limit human actions, while also allowing for the possibility that an individual may be able to negotiate a way to

---

[2] In fact, I began by studying four groups of students in different classes, eventually deciding to focus only on this year 11 class for a variety of reasons, one of them being their diverse cultural backgrounds.

break free from those constraints and from the moral orders that they consider to be unfair, immoral or personally limiting. And I want to know what role the media might play in shaping young people's conception of the world and their capacity to imagine different moral orders at a critical juncture in their lives.

Entering the field

So I'm on my way across town to find out how these girls, in the penultimate year of high school, are negotiating the conduct of their moral careers in relation to the competing moral orders that are presented to them by their family and the school as well as the popular media they encounter. In order to do this, I have established contact with the media teacher who is keen to have me assist her in the development of her media curriculum at the same time as I sit in on her lessons and participate in the student activities. I have talked to her about the project as a whole, and she understands that my purpose is to find out as much as I can about the role of the media in the girls' lives.

Over the course of the year, I will therefore engage in quite a bit of 'wild thinking', embracing an eclectic range of methods borrowed from sociology, anthropology, life history and education. This will include (and this is by no means an exhaustive list):

- An observation diary that I will keep for the entire year. In this I record daily encounters at the school as they happened, as well as my attempts to work towards more theoretical explanations of what I have observed at the end of the day. The latter I describe as 'reflective memos', following the methodology of sociologist Anselm Strauss (1987), although they might also be described as *introspections* to use Bausinger's term.
- A questionnaire about media preferences and habits distributed early in the year in a Friday afternoon class.
- The development of a unit of work on the films of American director John Hughes (*The Breakfast Club* (1985), *Pretty in Pink* (1986), and *Ferris Bueller's Day Off* (1986)). This afforded an opportunity to think through ideas about auteurship as well as genre (the teen film). The films also provoked a discussion of gender roles and expectations in school, and family life in the USA, with the girls being encouraged to make comparisons with their own experience in Australia.

- A unit of work on 'stars' – this culminated in each of the girls constructing a poster about a celebrity that mattered to them which they presented in class. This produced some memorable 'performances' of the self.
- An outing to a major television station in the city to give the girls a behind-the-scenes look at the production of a daily breakfast show. The girls were allowed to wear their own clothes instead of school uniform and to travel by public transport. The very different ways in which they responded and participated in this event were revelatory.
- We also devised an end-of-year video project, which, for a variety of reasons, was never fully achieved. However, one memorable script entitled *Wogs at Home* (a play on the then popular stage show *Wogs at Work*), was written by a group of girls who identified as Macedonian in terms of their nationality. This dealt with the disastrous repercussions of a teenage pregnancy in a Macedonian household.
- I also conducted a series of extended interviews with each of the girls – drawing on what I had learned about them and their media interests while encouraging them to reflect on their experiences of home, family and school as well as their hopes for the future in an *introspective* process.

By the end of the year, I had accumulated a large amount of data, the analysis of which was somewhat delayed by the fact that I was also pregnant. When I finally returned to the thesis after the birth of my son, it took a further year to sort and code this data into some form of manageable resource.

In order to do this, I employed a complex coding system as suggested by Anselm Strauss in his book *Qualitative Analysis for Social Scientists* (1987). This was the approach advocated for the handling of large volumes of qualitative data by the La Trobe sociologist Lyn Richards and her husband Tom, who were in the process of developing a computerized data management software programme called NUD∗IST (which stood for Non-Numerical Unstructured Data Indexing Searching and Theorising) that would evolve into the now world-standard platform, NVivo. In 1989 I attended a workshop run by Lyn and Tom that provided me with the conceptual (but unfortunately not the technological) tools to cross-code my data into the five main categories Media, Self, Family, School and Self Reflection. The latter being the category of comments where I reflected on my role as a researcher. Having 'fractured' the data and constructed an elaborate tree-structured index, I then wrote an individual 'media biography' for each of the girls. In writing up my final account, I was thus able to move from an analysis of the structural features of the girls' shared social context and media engagement to a discussion of their individual situations, which were unique.

As I discovered, one of the key determinants of each girl's social experience, and thus her relationship to the media, was her ethnic background and family life. In a class of twenty-two, there were five girls who identified as Anglo-Australian and six who identified as Macedonian, two girls identified as Portuguese, two as Yugoslavian and two as Polish. There was also one Spanish girl, one Italian, one Fijian-Indian, one Sri Lankan and one Lebanese, each with their own stories of family history and migration. The dominant group in the classroom, however, were the Macedonian girls who sat together at the back of the room. This group of vivacious teens, with their explosive clouds of back-combed hair, were the most voluble, the most argumentative and, inevitably, the most entertaining. They were also the ones who were most likely to hijack a media studies lesson in a way that I immediately connected to Michel de Certeau's concept of 'la perruque' or wig (1984, p. 25): this refers to the capacity of a worker to divert the time for which they are paid by their employer to personal work that is of more value to them. For example, while working on advertising as a topic early in the year, the girls were encouraged to produce their own TV commercials to demonstrate their understanding of the techniques used. This provided two of the Macedonian girls with a tactical opportunity to flaunt the school make-up ban by introducing an impressive quantity of cosmetics into the classroom. These they applied on camera, while ostensibly 'sending up' the extravagant claims of the manufacturers, before cheerfully heading off to their next lesson with a cast-iron excuse as to why they were so heavily made-up at school. As this incident revealed, the girls were well aware of the ways in which they were expected to be critical of the operations of the popular media when it came to advertising, but that did not prevent them from embracing the advertised commodities in a gleeful performance of their own identity.

It was, however, the poster-making exercise that was most illustrative of the ways in which the popular media supplied the girls with resources for the construction and performance of the self. Although the majority of the girls chose a male celebrity for their poster, these were hardly straightforward representations of masculinity given that they included the sexually ambiguous Robert Smith of British band The Cure, as well as the flamboyant George Michael and Boy George, neither of whom were 'out' in terms of their sexuality at that time. Only three girls chose a female star, with two choosing the then ascendant Madonna still in her 'virgin-whore' incarnation as their posters suggested. One girl, however, chose the American actress Joan Collins, then starring in the melodramatic drama series *Dynasty* (ABC 1981–89).

In explaining why she chose Robert Smith for her poster, Andy, one of the two Anglo-Australian girls in the class, explained that it was Smith's appearance and style that had encouraged her to adopt her new 'punk' haircut. This involved a close-cropped mop moulded into spikes that changed colour weekly. On the outing to the TV studio, Andy completed this look with tiny pieces of toilet paper stuck on each orange tip, a prank that revealed her capacity to send herself up for the amusement of others. However, as Andy reflected in her interview, her adoption of this style was a calculated refusal to embrace the more 'feminine' style adopted by the other girls in the class, and a statement of 'difference' in her desire to go on to art school. Andy's choice of Smith thus revealed how the popular media were providing the girls with a range of alternative resources with which to think about both their personal style, performance of self and the management of their moral careers. Yet in identifying what role the media might play in their choice of action and plans for the future there were many other factors that came into play, as was evident in the case of Leah.

A quiet and studious girl, Leah, who identified as Lebanese Catholic, was academically one of the most gifted and ambitious. As she informed me in our extended interview, she wanted to be a pharmacist despite the fact that her parents did not think there was much point in a girl pursuing a career. This was clearly evident in the fact that Leah was regularly absent from school. As the eldest of six children she was frequently needed to help out at home by her mother who had married and started a family at the age of 16. Leah's description of her home life included the detail that, while she and her siblings spoke Lebanese with their parents, they spoke English with each other. This language differentiation was underlined by the use of the family's two television sets. While the parents watched Lebanese films on one, Leah and her siblings were allowed to watch English-language programmes on the other. However, as a ritual of family solidarity, Leah's mother would record the American daytime soap opera *Days of Our Lives* (NBC 1965–) for the female members of the family to watch together in the evenings. As was evident from her comments, Leah loved her family even as she struggled to come to terms with the restrictions they placed on her movements outside the home and their expectations that she should leave school at 16, marry and start a family.

When asked to explain why she had chosen Joan Collins as her 'star', Leah initially suggested that this was simply a matter of convenience since there were many copies of *TV Week* lying around at home and Collins was a recurring presence. This was indeed true, but so was the young Kylie Minogue, then starring in *Neighbours*, as well as Madonna, the subject of two other girls' posters. It subsequently emerged that Leah claimed to admire Collins precisely because she was a successful *older* woman with a long career as a movie star and now a soap queen. Commenting on this long career in the context of Collins' multiple marriages and subsequent divorces, Leah suggested that Collins was someone who did not care what people thought of her. According to Leah, Collins was admirable because she defied the politics of shame that serve to keep women married and in their place. As became abundantly evident, Leah's 'reading' of Collins involved a projection of her own experience and concerns.

An attention to the politics of shame within the family was a recurring theme in Leah's discussion of her media use at home. For example, she described how she and her sisters were not allowed to go to the local shopping mall or to the cinema unchaperoned because her parents were worried that someone might start spreading 'rumours' about them that would damage their 'reputation'. Leah was clearly aware of the moral imperative that in order to find a suitable husband her reputation and her virginity should remain intact, although she thought this highly unfair.

Ironically, as a result of her somewhat restricted diet of family-friendly television, Leah had become an avid viewer of the popular sitcom *The Cosby Show* (NBC 1984–92). This she admired for its representation of a loving family presided over by a benign patriarch (as performed by the subsequently disgraced Bill Cosby). What impressed her about this aspirational middle-class family was the fact that the four daughters were expected to go to university and to countenance a career. However, while *The Cosby Show* and Joan Collins might offer Leah examples of how she might conduct her moral career differently, and the teachers at school were also encouraging her to pursue her studies, Leah appeared caught between her desire for a career and her love of family. It therefore came as no surprise to find out that Leah had left school midway through her final year to become a beautician.

Although this may indeed have constituted a positive step in the direction of a future career, it was not one that involved completing high school and a university qualification. Invited to sum up the role of the media in her life, Leah confessed that it played a 'big part' and that she would be lost without it. She described herself as being 'addicted' to television because it was her way of 'seeing the outside world' and how other people live, given that she accepted the fact that she would never have the opportunity to experience this for herself.

I've chosen to focus on the story of Leah here as an example of the complexity of the competing forces operational in the lives of *all* the girls that I interviewed. In terms of their moral careers, while their teachers may have been advocating the importance of academic effort in order to achieve independence and a career, their family obligations were often pulling them in a different direction. Meanwhile, the media they encountered were offering them a whole set of other possibilities that had the potential to shape their view of the world and possibly their future course of action. However, as became evident during the course of my research, it was impossible to talk about the role of the media in the girls' lives without reference to the other dimensions of their social experience at that time and in that place.

On reflection

This, then, was the research experience that has continued to inform my thinking about 'the why', 'the how', 'the when' and 'the where' of media audience research. In terms of 'the why', I initially embarked on the study of how young people might relate to the media because I was curious about the role of the media in the lives of the students that I had been teaching. As a teacher and as a postgraduate researcher, I wanted to explore, and to test, the prevailing view that the popular media were of little value and to find a more nuanced way of understanding how young people might relate to the wide range of media they encountered and the kinds of value it might hold for them. In terms of 'the how', my approach was to select a group of girls in a secondary school and to effectively define them as an audience for the purpose of my study even though I regarded them first and foremost as people. As history reveals, given that people so often practise their media audiencing in private, the media audience that becomes the focus of research is almost always a construction, summoned into existence by the design of the research project itself. The 'when' and the 'where' were both a function of the opportunities afforded to me at a particular moment as a postgraduate student and teacher. The choice of the school in the western suburbs and the connection with the media teacher and her classes were the result of a helpful suggestion from one of my colleagues in the Graduate School of Education: in effect, this was a matter of chance.

Perhaps the most important question to be answered is therefore what was the value of this research? To which the answer is inevitably somewhat convoluted since this study involved so many people over a period of time. On a personal level, it was of value in a number of different ways: it enabled me to qualify for the award of a doctoral degree and advance my academic career while providing me with valuable research insights which I was able to publish and share with others. Indeed, it has subsequently enabled me to advocate a more nuanced understanding of young people's relationship to the popular media and the value that this may for them and I have published a number of essays related to this project over the years (Turnbull, 1993, 1998a, 1998b). As a project, it continues to be of relevance, since many years later I am revisiting my findings in the context of a new study that considers the role of television in the history of migration to Australia. Contact has been made with two of the women from the original study and I will be interviewing them once again to explore their reflections on their experience growing up with television in Australia.[3] This is knowledge that will be shared in the usual academic ways, through presentations at conferences, through the publication of papers and books, all of which may have a particular kind of value in terms of an academic career. However, and this is the larger question that I have been pondering: what is the value of audience research to those whom we research?

In the current research environment, there is an increasing focus on engagement and impact. In Australia, as in the UK, there are now reporting systems in place that require academics to account for the value of their research to society at large. My own university defines research impact as:

---

[3]This is an Australian Research Linkage Project entitled 'Migration, Cultural Diversity and Television: Reflecting Modern Australia', with researchers Professor Kate Darian-Smith, Senior Professor Sue Turnbull and Dr Sukhmani Khorana; our Linkage Partners are the Australian Centre for the Moving Image and Museum Victoria, LP150100202.

the contribution that research makes to the economy, society, environment and culture *beyond* the contribution to academic research.[4]

While research engagement is defined as:

> the interaction between researchers and research end-users *outside of academia* for the mutually beneficial transfer of knowledge, technologies, methods or resources.[5]

As these two definitions reveal, academics are now being asked to justify their research in terms of the broader societal benefits that will accrue to the 'end-users'. Examples of 'end-users' offered include 'an individual, community or organization external to academia that will directly use or directly benefit from the output, outcome or result of the research'.[6] While these definitions are intended to encompass research conducted in both the sciences and the humanities, what is not mentioned are the potential benefits that may accrue to the individuals who may participate in the process of the research that we may conduct.

For example, when I reflect on the research described, I now wonder what value it might have had for the girls who were the participants since they hardly qualify as 'end-users'. For a start, they had no say in their decision to participate, since in the then current research environment, less rigorous than today's, the only approval I needed in order to gain access to them was that of the then headmistress of the school. As far as their media teacher was concerned, my research project may have been of some value to her since, as the only media teacher in the school, she was otherwise isolated. As well as providing her with some ideas for the development of the curriculum, over the course of the year we became firm allies in our conviction that a critical study of the popular media could be both enjoyable and productive. But what about the girls themselves?

Clearly there was much enjoyment and amusement to be had in the media studies classroom for which I was only partially responsible in the design of some of the tasks. Looking back over my record of the year, I can recall many moments of great hilarity, but also moments of revelation. This was particularly true in the poster exercise that I

---

[4] https://intranet.uow.edu.au/raid/era/engagement-impact/

[5] Ibid; my italics.

[6] Ibid.

devised, when girls talked about their attachment to a particular star, as well as in the interviews when they were encouraged to engage in a form of *introspection* about their media tastes and practices. Introspection, it will be recalled, was one of the methodological tools suggested by Hermann Bausinger as being of potential value in the study of the media in the practice of everyday life, although I suspect he may have been talking about the self-reflexivity of the researcher rather than the researched. That being said, providing the girls with the opportunity to reflect on their media practices and their attachments through a process of introspection may well have been a valuable exercise in and of itself since this constituted an opportunity for them to achieve self-understanding.

This was clearly evident in the transcripts of the interviews that I undertook with each of the girls towards the end of the year; some of the interviews were over an hour long. Conducted in the school councillor's office, a space which the girls evidently associated with self-revelation and confession, these interviews provided an opportunity for the girls to talk about themselves, their hopes, their dreams for the future as well as well as their attachments to the media. These interviews were often breathtaking in their honesty and impossible to effectively summarize. The challenge for me as a researcher was therefore to produce an account of the girls' varied media practices that could do justice to them as individuals while providing my academic readership with some insight into the girls' experience as 'an audience' in a particular place and time. What I did not offer at that time was any feedback to the girls that might have been of value to them personally. In effect, their story became my story in an act of appropriation.

Which brings me back to the 'why' of media audience research. As the history of media audience research reveals, this may be undertaken for a variety of reasons by a variety of stakeholders, including the media industries themselves, government, academic and other researchers whose motivations may differ wildly. Many people want to know about audiences, including advertisers, market researchers, broadcasters and content producers across the entire spectrum of available media. Inevitably, most of the research undertaken in these various fields is conducted by those who begin their career in some form of academic training where they will encounter what has been written about audiences by those who have researched them over the years. When it comes to academic audience research within the field of media and communication, what they are likely to encounter is research that has been prompted by curiosity and interest, anxiety and concern, or a desire to rescue and defend the practices of the audience in question. So when I consider 'the why' of academic media audience research today, I think it is imperative to think about what purpose it will serve. While I have no problem with the fact that undertaking and publishing research is an imperative for those seeking to advance their career, I think there is good reason for thinking about the engagement and impact factors that may benefit not just the end-users of such research, but also the participants. In other words, how can we increase the value of our research to those whom we study?

Looking forward, looking back

In his evaluation of the field of audience research in 2006, provocatively entitled 'I Have Seen the Future and It Is Not Here Yet ...; or, On Being Ambitious for Audience Research', Martin Barker suggested that there are two main drivers of academic audience research. While the first of these has been a desire 'to rescue' an audience, or its chosen media, from obscurity of misunderstanding, another might be that an issue about audiences had become a 'problem' for our belief system in some way. In other words, audience researchers would appear to be driven either by altruism or by a desire to investigate that which bothers them or society at large. While these are good reasons for undertaking audience research, Barker's point is that, in his opinion, the field has become 'stuck' at what he describes as 'the level of accumulation'. What, he asks, are our ambitions for the field? What are the kinds of questions we want to be able to ask and answer? In seeking to answer his own question, Barker suggests that in his opinion we need to look at the history of media audience research, including what he defines as the latter days of the 'uses and gratifications' theory in the 1970s, in its attempt to combine, in a mutually informative way, a theoretical framework, working concepts, methods of enquiry, research implements and paradigmatic studies.

While critically derided for its essentially functionalist approach, uses and gratifications research, as advocated by Jay Blumler and Elihu Katz (1974), proposed that people took from the media what was useful to them. As Ross and Nightingale suggest, this approach shifted attention away from the content of the media to focus directly on the audience, 'stressing the use of the media to satisfy social and psychological needs' (Ross and Nightingale, 2003, p. 29). The problem with this approach, they argue, is that it has low explanatory power since both social and psychological needs are context specific. At its best, uses and gratifications research can therefore only offer an 'individualistic' explanation of audience behaviours. Nevertheless, as Ross and Nightingale point out, the 'uses and gratifications' approach was the first to champion the notion of 'the active audience', shifting emphasis from what the media does to people to what people do with the media (Ross and Nightingale, 2003, p. 31). In their opinion, the problem here is that this instrumental approach inevitably plays down the connection of media research to social theory, opting instead for a study of motivations derived from the field of social psychology. But, as I will argue, it doesn't have to. It is quite possible to maintain a focus on the members of an audience while also drawing on larger concepts to explain their engagement with the media in ways that do indeed draw on, or even advance, social theory.

For example, as I discovered in the research project described, how people account for their media practices usually reveals the perceived moral orders and/or social constraints that may pertain in any social context. That is, when asked to account for their media audience practices, people will seek to justify these with reference to their lived experience of a specific social and cultural context as well as the relevant hierarchies of taste. For example, explaining one's engagement in watching a series such as *Ru Paul's Drag Race* (Logo 2009–16; VH1 2017–) may well be complicated by a perception of how one might be judged for being a fan, not only by those asking the question but society at large. One of the goals of media audience research is therefore to understand what the practice of being part of a media audience looks like from the perspective of those who engage in it. The challenge for the researcher then becomes finding a way to map this landscape in ways that make it intelligible. But is this enough?

This brings me once again to the question of the value of media audience research and a number of key questions that I want to raise in the current context, all of which relate to the question of value:

> What is the value of media audience research to those who are the object of the research? To society at large? To the researchers who undertake it?

And

> What is the value of the media experience/practice to those who are engaged in it and how best can audience researchers account for this?

These are the questions that I shall seek to address in the following pages in which I take up Barker's challenge to consider the history of media audience research in order to find a way forward. There are great riches to be found and much to be learned from the questions that have been asked, the approaches embraced and lessons learned that can help inform our understanding of the ways in which people practise their audiencing today.

The scope of this book

What I offer here is very far from a complete history of media audience research. There are already excellent collections that accomplish this in greater depth and detail, including Andy Ruddock's *Understanding Audiences* (2001) and Virginia Nightingale's more recent edited collection, *The Handbook of Media Studies* (2014). When considering audiences from the perspective of the media industries, the foundational work of Ien Ang in *Desperately Seeking the Audience* (1991), Tom O'Regan and Mark Balnaves in *Rating the Audience* (2012) and James G. Webster in *The Marketplace of Attention* (2014), as well as Phillip Napoli's analysis of the evolving digital landscape in *Audience Evolution* (2010), offer invaluable insights into this particular branch of audience research. Nor will I deal in any depth with the burgeoning field of fan studies that has emerged over the last 30 years, although the notion of the active audience on which this depends has been central to my own research over the years. Once again, there are excellent texts and collections already devoted to this field (see Gray et al., 2017). Inevitably this book therefore reflects my own ongoing interests in television as the medium with which I grew up and which I continue to study as it evolves into online content, and the digital landscape in which my current students now operate. What follows is therefore a 'guided tour' through the complex history of media audience research that has brought me to the conclusion that the most illuminating audience studies are those that conceive of the audience as people leading complex lives who bring to their media experience a wealth of knowledge and experience that will inevitably shape how they respond to whatever it is that they encounter there. The larger question I want to pose and to which I shall return to in the end, is what value media audience research might have not only for those who undertake it but also those who participate.

Chapter 2 therefore begins with a discussion of how the media audience has been defined over time in order to illuminate some of the patterns that have emerged. Indeed, perhaps one of the most frustrating aspects of media audience research is the way in which new media forms continue to provoke long-standing anxieties and the same questions. This is also revealed in Chapter 3, which considers media audience research that originates with a concern about the impact of a specific media technology. Chapter 4 reflects on the kinds of content that have continued to motivate audience research, including an obsession with sex and violence. Chapter 5 returns to the question of exactly who has been studied and why, since it is clear that some audiences have received much more attention than others. Chapter 6 considers the kinds of method that have been used, their promise and their limitations in the interests of inspiring a new generation of media audience researchers to think in new ways about the kinds of 'audiencing' in which people engage today and how best to study this. However, rather than being a 'how to' guide, since there are already many such texts available (see Brennen, 2017), this chapter returns to a consideration of the ways in which the audience has been conceptualized for the purposes of research and will once again return to the question of value.

2 What is a Media Audience?

Let's start with a question. What do you think of when you hear the term 'media audience'? What image pops into your mind? Is it the stock photo of a nuclear family sitting round a television set watching a programme in their living room (see Illustration 2.1)?

Is it people watching a film at the cinema (see Illustration 2.2)?

Is it people reading a newspaper on a train (see Illustration 2.3)?

All of these activities, and many more, have been identified as media audience practices in relation to what is now described as 'legacy' media. This would include the printed newspaper or magazine, listening to the radio or watching television, and a trip to the local cinema. The major difference being that we can now access all of that content on a hand-held device, anywhere and anytime, providing we have the funds to acquire the right technology and a reliable internet connection. As Adam Greenfield has observed in his book *Radical Technologies: The Design of Everyday Life* (2017), smartphones have indeed 'altered the texture' of people's lives all over the world in extraordinary ways, transforming everyday rituals as well as people's relationship to the spaces which they inhabit: spaces in which they can now be part of a media audience anywhere and anytime.

Reliable internet connectivity, however, is by no means a given in many parts of the world, leading to what has been described as a 'digital divide' that separates more affluent communities from those who are less privileged. The speed with which audiences can access content can also varies considerably. In 2018, it was estimated that while Singapore had the fastest broadband speed in the world at 60.39 megabits per second, the United States came in at number 20 at 25.86 megabits per second, while Australia, where I live, on the other hand, did not even make it into the top 50.[1] So while some societies have invested

---

[1] Chisato Goya, 'The 23 countries in the world with the fastest internet speeds', *Business Insider*, July 24, 2018, https://www.businessinsider.com/the-23-countries-in-the-world-with-the-fastest-internet-speeds-2018-7/?r=AU&IR=T/#23-france-2423-megabits-per-second-1

22 Media Audiences

Illustration 2.1 Family viewing – although in this image the TV has yet to be switched on
Credit: Blue Jean Images/Alamy Stock Photo.

Illustration 2.2 A cinema audience in waiting
Credit: Directphoto Collection/Alamy Stock Photo.

in a 'fast' broadband network, there are those who have only invested in a relatively 'slow' one. These are the kinds of technological and practical issues that will inevitably impact on the experience of being part of an audience.

Despite such global variations, many people across the world now have access to digital devices that enable them to consume, and also to produce and share, different kinds of media content every day. As a

Illustration 2.3 How people used to read the news on the train
Credit: Gregory Wrona/Alamy Stock Photo.

Illustration 2.4 Family viewing in the internet connected home
Credit: ONOKY – Photononstop/Alamy Stock Photo.

result, your image of the family in front of the television might well look somewhat different. While the family may be together in the one space in front of the TV, they may also be using their own mobile devices for a variety of purposes (see Illustration 2.4).

It might be noted, that despite the difference in time and space, this stock image is of a very white, nuclear Western family in what looks like a pretty affluent home. Many 'families' are not like this. As for the newspaper readers on the subway, these days people sitting in the silent carriage of a train are more likely to be reading the news they want to read on their mobile phones on a platform of their own choosing. People are no longer reading the same select number of newspapers or watching the same network news broadcasts. In fact, the people on the train may be watching a movie, television show, looking at their social media platforms, doing their banking or playing a game (see Illustration 2.5).

But let's pause for a moment and consider that although we are living at a time when the ways in which people access information and entertainment are rapidly changing there may still be occasions when we prefer to buy a printed newspaper or a magazine; families may still choose to gather together around the largest screen in the house for a television event; and friends may still want to go to the cinema together to see a film.

Indeed, the return of the vinyl record and portable record-player suggest that there may be aspects of the legacy media that audiences today are keen to hang on to, despite the convenience of that converged media device in their pocket or bag. While this might be a form of nostalgia, as the history of media technologies reveals, the arrival of any new media form or technology rarely involves a radical break with the past. Usually, this entails a rather more gradual process of evolution

Illustration 2.5 Audiencing on a train?
Credit: Simon Dack/Alamy Stock Photo.

and adaptation as people discover just what the affordances of the 'new' media they encounter might be, whether they want to access these – if they can afford to buy them – and how best to use them in the context of their own lives. Inevitably this involves a process of working out the value of a new technology and what purposes it might best serve.

Perhaps even more importantly, audiences today are no longer merely consumers of content, if they ever were, but also *produsers*, to employ Axel Bruns' portmanteau term to signal how *users* of the media now have the capacity to *produce* their own media (Bruns, 2008, p. 21). Reflecting on the history of media audiences, it is, however, important to note that audiences have always been productive in a variety of ways, not least in the production of meaning. More specifically, it is important to think about readers' letters to newspapers and magazines, or the production of fan magazines and fan fiction or even various forms of cultural tourism which have a very long history indeed. What has changed is the capacity 'to publish' and share these audience-produced materials in a digital form on easily accessible media platforms such as YouTube with relative ease, as will be discussed in more detail in Chapter 4. As Philip Napoli has pointed out, user-generated content now competes with traditional media content for audience attention (Napoli, 2010, p. 1). But how do we research such audience activities?

Mapping the media manifold

For example, as I write this, I am sitting in a café working on my laptop surrounded by people, most of whom have mobile phones in their hands. Some of them are looking at the screens, which cast a luminous glow over their faces as they sip their coffee, but I can't tell what they are seeing without peering over their shoulder and everyone 'knows' this would not be a good idea. It would, in fact, be perceived as extremely rude and intrusive, pointing to the fact that there are indeed social protocols around mobile phone use, just as there have been for every other form of media technology in the past. While once this might have involved a debate about whether it is polite to leave the television set on when a guest arrives, now it is more likely to be on the acceptability of having a conversation on your mobile phone in public. Indeed, in some countries, such as Japan, this is banned on public transport, while other countries, including Australia where I live, have introduced quiet carriages on trains to try and contain the babble.

Perhaps the people in the coffee shop are checking their Facebook feed as a form of social interaction? Perhaps they are consulting the weather or the news, messaging a friend or checking their emails before they get to work? Perhaps someone is playing a digital game, on their own or with others? One of the senior academics at my university can be regularly observed playing online word games with her son as she waits for meetings to begin. This online activity therefore functions as a means for mother and son to stay in touch: a kind of mothering at a distance.

While a word game might seem a bit old-fashioned, someone in the coffee shop might be scouting the location of their next Pokémon Go target. As a 'locative' game employing augmented reality, Pokémon Go enables players to 'see' virtual creatures or Pokémon on their phone, using their camera's video and GPS capacities. People are then inspired to pursue and 'catch' a virtual Pokémon in their own location by swiping an online ball across it on their screen. This constitutes a 'doubling of place' – the location of the player in 'real' space being overlaid by a 'digital' space in which they can also operate. Sometimes the two may collide in unfortunate ways. For example, while standing in Euston Station in London in October 2016 at the height of the Pokémon Go craze, I saw a large sign asking people to be mindful of others while chasing Pokémon and to make sure they did not fall off the platform or onto the rails in their eagerness to capture a Squirtle. Apparently, Pokémon Go was so popular at this time that daily traffic exceeded that for other well-known media platforms such as Facebook and Twitter (Isbister, 2016).

There are other possible uses for the smartphone. In 2017, I conducted a very non-scientific random study amongst a group of visiting students from Hong Kong in which I asked them to form groups and list all the different uses they had for their smartphones. The winning group identified 42 different uses, including 'checking the news' and 'watching YouTube'. As was revealed by this tally, only a few of the functions could be classed as 'audience' activities; that is, the receiving of some form of content that has been shared in some way. For the most part, the students were using their phones as a kind of multipurpose digital Swiss army knife. As a woman who often travels alone (and the gender issue is significant), I frequently use my phone as a means of avoiding unwanted social interaction or the gaze of others. In this case, the mediated content is of far less significance than the use of the technology itself. As all these different functions and activities converge, it is extremely difficult to determine exactly who is part of a media audience even before we get to the issue of how this might be of significance for them.

Media audience research now encompasses an extensive field that inevitably includes the ways in which we use the media in everyday life. As anthropologist Elisabeth Bird notes, the notion of the 'audience' has become problematic precisely because the media have become so firmly enmeshed in what she describes as 'the web of culture': the audience is now both 'everywhere and nowhere' (Bird, 2003, p. 3). Media sociologist Nick Couldry would agree, arguing that in order to understand what he describes as the 'media manifold' in which people are embedded, a 'media-centric approach will serve us poorly' (Couldry, 2014, p. 226). What Couldry proposes instead is an 'open-minded, practice-based approach to whatever it is that people are doing with, or around media' (Couldry, 2014, p. 226). This suggests that we need to think very carefully what we mean by the term 'media audience' and the practice of 'audiencing'.

The etymology of the audience

Part of the problem has to do with the concept of an audience more broadly. Etymologically, the word derives from the present participle *audiens* of the Latin verb *audire*, which means 'listening' or 'hearing'. By the late 14th century, the word 'audience' in the English language had come to mean a 'formal hearing or reception', as in the still current notion of an 'audience with' a member of the royal family or a religious leader. By the 15th century, this meaning had been extended to include 'persons within hearing range' or 'an assembly of listeners'. Note that in these instances the concept of the audience was predicated on the sense of hearing rather than on seeing, even though it has been the sense of sight (and the dangers of 'looking') that have come to dominate so much thinking (and indeed anxiety) about media audiences over the last one hundred years.

Implicit within the early uses of the term, the concept of an audience connoted a notion of co-presence, of people listening and looking together in one space, such as people gathered together for a concert or a theatrical performance. In 1855, however, the term audience began to be used (experience suggests that in any form of scholarship it is always dangerous to claim a 'first') to refer to the readers of a book, marking a considerable shift in the notion of the audience, since it is at this point that the audience 'disappears' from view. Instead, the audience is now 'imagined' as an unspecified number of people who might never have any direct contact one with another. What unites them is the shared experience of the same mediated content, although their engagement with the book would most likely be in private in the comfort of their own home. It is at this moment, when media audiences start to disappear from public view, that anxieties about media effects also begin to emerge and the desire to find out what is going on becomes paramount.

The fact that so many media audience activities occur in private and unobserved has presented a considerable challenge to media audience research over the years, although inventive measures have been devised for trying to discover what audiences are up to. This has included quantifiable measures such as distribution figures, radio or TV ratings and surveys, as well as more qualitative measures such as participant observation interviews and focus groups. None of these methods, however, are entirely without problems since they usually involve some form of interpretation and/or self-reporting. With regard to the latter, people may have many different reasons for how they wish to present their media activities. For example, it has long been known that people tend to overestimate their attention to the news and current affairs while underestimating the time they devote to entertainment. When it comes to the media audience studies that involve observable behaviour, how that behaviour might be accounted for may entail complex issues of interpretation on the part of the observer that may misrepresent what is actually going on.

Audiencing in practice

These days 'audiencing', as suggested by cultural studies scholar John Fiske (1992) is something that can be done alone, in the company of strangers, like-minded others or together with family and friends, both in person or online. There are, in fact, many ways in which people can choose how they wish to be part of an audience, depending on their inclination and their immediate location in time and space. Indeed, there is a social and experiential dimension to 'audiencing' that may well be one of the reasons people choose to engage in the activity in the first place. The social experience of being with friends, family or a group of like-minded others in a shared mediated event is still a key driver of our media audience activities. Indeed, there are many media events that are designed to cater specifically to this social need, including reality TV shows such as the global franchise *Big Brother*, which first appeared in the Netherlands in 1999, as well as more recent manifestations such as *Married at First Sight*, which was the highest-rating show on free-to-air television in April 2019 in Australia.[2]

Although there is no doubt that media technologies and the content people consume and produce are continuing to evolve and change, the *needs* which the media will meet, the *uses* to they will be put and the *value* that people derive from the audience experience may not have changed as much as might be expected. For some time now I have been tempted to rewrite American psychologist Abraham Maslow's hierarchy of human needs, first published in 1943,[3] as a hierarchy of media functions. People continue to use the media for information, for finding things out; for entertainment, fun, distraction and consolation; and for all the various aspects of identity formation and social activity that go along with looking for recognition, support and self-expression. While 'fun', as Alan McKee points out, has long been completely undervalued and untheorized as a 'central organising principle of entertainment' (McKee, 2016, p. 2).

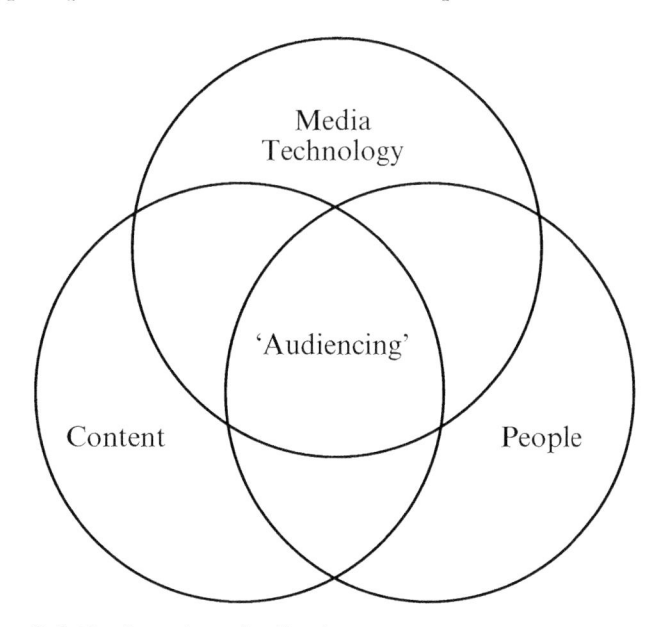

Figure 2.1 The dimensions of audiencing

---

[2]https://mumbrella.com.au/married-at-first-sight-finds-new-series-high-with-1-685m-metro-viewers-571249

[3]Hannah Blackiston, 'Married at First Sight Hits New Rating High', Mumbrella, March 25, 2019, https://www.psychologytoday.com/blog/hide-and-seek/201205/our-hierarchy-needs, accessed 29 April 2019

In an endeavour to define what is encompassed by the practice of media audiencing, I want to argue that there are 'still' three dimensions to the audience experience that we need to take into account (Figure 2.1).

The first involves the use of a media device or technology, whatever that might be. The second involves some form of shareable content, produced either by an established media company or by anyone with the impulse to take advantage of a Web 2.0 environment that allows people to create and upload their own media content to the Internet, where it can be accessed by others. The third involves the people who participate in this mediated experience who may or may not come together in real time in order to do so. For example, the audience for a globally available media product like the HBO drama series *Game of Thrones* may be widely dispersed in both time and place. Indeed, there is not just one media audience for *Game of Thrones* but many, whether this be a group of friends who discuss the show online or a person watching the DVD who is aware that in so doing they are participating in a global audience experience. It is therefore possible for someone watching *Game of Thrones* to 'imagine' themselves as being part of an audience that they know exists without ever meeting anyone else who watches the show. Furthermore, it is quite possible for a researcher to construct an audience research project that involves people who watch the show who may never meet in real time. Media audiences are, as a result, often 'imagined' constructs, especially in everyday discourse when people talk about the 'global' audience for *Game of Thrones*.

As far as the media industries themselves are concerned, media audiences matter because their economic viability depends on monetizing these audiences in some way, whether this be at point of sale or as a commodity that can in turn be sold to advertisers. For example, there are now commercial media companies that trawl the Internet looking for 'mentions' of shows like *Game of Thrones* on social media sites such as Facebook. This information is then sold to those who want to reach this audience for commercial purposes of their own. In this way, knowledge about media audiences, where they are located and how to access them is worth a great deal of money.

Audience economics

According to media economist Philip Napoli, we are in the midst of an 'audience evolution', a biological metaphor that once again suggests not so much a break with the past as a gradual process of change. As they evolve, audiences are not only changing what they do, but the industry is also changing in order to keep up with them (Napoli, 2010, p. 4). In a report entitled, 'Screen Wars: The Battle for Eye Space in a TV-Everywhere World', the Nielsen company, which has a long history of involvement in audience measurement across the globe, quotes Executive Vice President Megan Clarken on why the media industry needs to embrace the changing media in order to adapt their strategies 'to fit with this new reality, offering engaging and relevant content that is easily accessible across devices and channels' (Nielsen, 2015a).

The key imperative here is the perceived need 'to understand' consumer behaviour rather than simply the desire to track or capture it. At which point it might be worth noting that the subtitle to this report is 'Desperately Seeking the Audience Around the World' – an intentional or unintentional reference to Australian academic Ien Ang's influential analysis of the challenges facing the media industries in their efforts to capture people's engagement with the media, originally published in 1991.

This Nielsen (2015b) report goes on to elucidate the findings from the company's Nielsen Global Digital Landscape Survey that polled 30,000 online respondents in 60 countries to help in 'understanding' the changing digital landscape. What it discovered was both surprising and somewhat predictable. According to its data, 65 per cent of global respondents still prefer to watch video programming 'live', at its regularly scheduled time. It might be noted that video programing in this context is defined as any type of content, such as TV, cable shows, professional video or user-generated content that is watched on a TV, PC, laptop, mobile phone, tablet or e-reader device. More than half of the respondents (53 per cent) suggested that the reason they liked to keep up with 'live programming' was so they could 'join in the conversation on social media'. With this objective in mind, 47 per cent of the global respondents confirmed that they engaged with social media while watching.

These statistics are somewhat less surprising if we note that this survey was carried out online, presumably with people who had access to the technologies and connectivity that enabled them to be online in the first place and were therefore much more likely to be online while watching. This possibility the report acknowledges, arguing that in developing markets where online penetration is still growing, audiences may be both younger and more affluent than the rest of the population in that culture. Furthermore, it is admitted, the statistics quoted were based on what people 'claimed' they did rather than on actual 'metered' behaviour. This is an important caveat since this online poll inevitably ignores the less affluent, those in remote locations with poor online connectivity and the elderly or very young who have limited access to digital technologies. The poor, the very young and the old have long been the least attractive audiences for the commercial media industries to reach, given their limited spending power. Not all audiences are created equal.

While this Nielsen (2015a) report suggests that watching television on a television screen might be the preferred platform across all generations, it also reveals that this practice is most common amongst older consumers. This includes those identified as belonging to the 'The Silent Generation (ages 65+)', 'Baby Boomers (ages 50–64)' and 'Generation X (ages 35–49)'. Watching television on a television is, however, lowest amongst 'Generation Z (ages 15–20)' and 'Millennials (ages 21–34)'. We might note the absence of children under the age of 15 in this analysis, a group that might tentatively be identified as the iPad generation who prefer their personal screens to any other.

If the goal of the television industry is to produce content that delivers the most desirable audiences to those seeking to sell something to them, they clearly have their work cut out in more ways than one. According to this survey, two thirds of the global respondents suggested that they would switch to another television station in order to avoid the commercials. Sixty-four per cent of those surveyed admitted that they also downloaded programmes in order to avoid the 'advertising clutter' in their lives. Audiences, in other words, are actively trying to avoid those who are trying to capture their attention. In the television industry, this has resulted in major problems for the free-to-air commercial networks as audiences seek out subscription channels, streamed content and alternative forms of access where they can hopefully evade the advertising messages. Audiences are now driving change in the digital TV market (Lotz, 2014; Lobato, 2019).

What is also not so surprising about the Nielsen survey is the evidence that people watch television in order to be able to talk about it with other people, as was clearly the case with the *Big Brother* franchise, which became a global phenomenon in the first decade of the 21st century. People tuned in to this reality TV show and the many others that emerged, even when they didn't particularly like them, in order to join in the conversation about the events unfolding in these shows, either in person around the apocryphal water-cooler or online. The global *Big Brother* phenomenon incidentally inspired a whole raft of audience studies concerned with the impact, role and function of *Big Brother* for the franchise's avid global audience (Hill, 2005; Mathjis and Jones, 2004). What these studies revealed was that far from being a 'private' experience located in the home, watching television could be a highly social event given that it functioned as a form of social currency: a proposition that is as true of television when it was first introduced as it is today.

The advice Nielsen has to offer the media industry is therefore salutary. Video programming content producers need to engage with social media and become 'second screen' savvy. The media industries need to find new ways to connect with viewers across all of their devices in order to maximize the opportunity for exposure. Exposure, however, may no longer be the name of the game. As Philip Napoli argues, we are in the era of 'the attention economy'. In order to measure this attention and because contemporary audiences are 'spread across a much wider range of content options' and a 'much wider range of delivery platforms', in Napoli's opinion the media industries need to find much larger samples in order to 'accurately and reliably ascertain the distribution of audience attention' (Napoli, 2010, p. 6). Increased audience autonomy has therefore led to the need for new audience information systems that offer much more than simple metrics, systems that can 'mine' the data that is appearing in the online environment where audiences now engage with content in a wide variety of ways.

Take Sysomos, a data analysis company (based in New York) that promised in its online self-promotion 'access to the social media conversations' that will reveal 'what's happening, why it's happening, and who's driving the conversation' so that those seeking exposure can 'Discover the people and conversations that matter most to your brand' (https://sysomos.com/). As part of its suite of services, Sysomos offered advanced 'social listening tools' through the provision of Sysomos Map, a search engine for social media which allows the customer to type in a key word that will present 'instant results', including the reach and context of the topic both 'today' and 'historically'. Needless to say, this form of 'listening in' is taking place without the knowledge or the consent of those who are being listened in on. The use of such 'big data' is not without its ethical implications.

Concerning the audience

However, while economic interests have driven a great deal of media audience research over time, there have been many other drivers. These include an interest in the potential civic or educational value the media may offer, as well as a concern about the perceived positive or negative moral and social effects. Indeed, as history reveals, moral concerns about the imagined effects of the media have underpinned a great deal of media audience research. From the remarkable Payne Fund Studies conducted in the 1920s, motivated by anxieties about the moral and social impact of the motion picture industry on a cinema-going public (Jowett et al., 1996, Turnbull 1997), to more recent concerns about the effects of playing video games or of babies watching tablet computers. As David Buckingham (2003) and Sonia Livingstone (2009) have argued, children and young people have been perceived as particularly vulnerable audiences over time. Often such concerns also encompass anxieties about health and social well-being, and studies on them may be undertaken by government agencies with a view to introducing various forms of regulation and control that are perceived to be in the public interest.

In terms of the potential social effects, as has long been recognized, every new media technology or form is usually greeted by a combination of excitement and dread. From a utopian perspective, new media may be welcomed because of the presumed benefit they are likely to bring to society. This would include such noble aspirations as the ways in which the media might contribute to the education and enlightenment of the populace, with the potential to help bring about a more democratic and just society. At the same time there will also be those who will project a dystopian future in which this new media technology will result in social harm, adversely affecting the individual, their family and even whole cultures and communities in the process. This is as true today in the era of portable digital devices and their multiple applications as it was in the era of the printing press. While in the 19th century this might have involved concerns about uneducated working-class audiences consuming sensational news broadsheets that catered to their baser instincts, these days it might well involve worries about 'fake news'.

Underpinning these anxieties is the concept of causality – the idea that one thing causes another to happen. Causality has been an ongoing issue in media audience research because it implies that something (the media) is the direct cause of something else (has an effect) on people's behaviour. To offer a very familiar false causality in the history of media audience research, the fact that someone has watched a particular film may be cited as the cause of their criminal actions. This was famously the case in the Port Arthur Massacre in Australia in 1996 when newspapers suggested that the killer Martin Bryant had been inspired to mass murder by watching horror films such as *Child's Play 3* (1991). In fact, the motivations behind the actions of Bryant were extremely complex, and evidence offered by the forensic psychiatrist at his trial revealed that far from Bryant being a demented fan of horror films his favourite movie was the Disney animated feature *The Lion King* (1994). As this evidence suggested, Bryant was an extremely troubled young man of limited intellectual capacity who had been deeply affected by the suicide of his father (Turnbull, 1998).

Central to the problem of causality is the way in which the relationship between the media and the audience is framed. To ask the question:

What effect does this media (whichever or whatever it is) have on these people (whomever or wherever they are)?

has never been helpful since it implicitly assumes that the media is the agent responsible for the effect. The more useful approach necessitates turning the question around to ask more open questions such as:

What role does this mediated experience play in people's lives?

At which point we might add another significant question:

How do I as a researcher account for this?

As has already been suggested, academic audience research may also be driven by curiosity and an openness to discovery. There is a considerable difference between 'looking for' an answer to a specific question or issue in relation to a media audience and 'looking at' a media audience in a spirit of genuine curiosity. This is not to suggest that such curiosity-driven research is entirely disinterested or value free, since every researcher brings to the task their own interpretative framework that will inevitably impact on the ways in which they construct the research project and account for what they perceive. This is clearly evident in the branch of academic research known as 'fan studies' that has played a significant role in drawing attention to the active and creative engagement of audiences with specific media texts. While much of this research has been driven by genuine curiosity, over the years it has also served as a form of advocacy on behalf of the positive benefits such audience engagement might have.

For example, although by no means the first to undertake a study of fan engagement with a text, in 1992 American academic Henry Jenkins set out in his book *Textual Poachers* to recuperate the image of the fan as lonely obsessed 'fanatic'. Revealing himself to be both an academic and a fan of the American TV series *Star Trek*, Jenkins was eager to demonstrate just how active, creative and community oriented the fan experience might be. Many years later, in a study of the fans for the HBO series *Game of Thrones*, (Finn, 2017) the focus is once again on the communities created by the book and the television series. In this edited book, which is part of the University of Chicago series entitled Fan Phenomena, the various authors are again concerned with the ways in which these various communities 'envision themselves as consumers, critics, and even creators of fanworks in a wide variety of media including fiction, art, fancasting and cosplay'.[4]

Framing the audience

As is evident from the brief overview given, there are many different reasons for conducting an audience research project and many different ways of framing the audience for the purposes of research. This suggests that if presented with an example of media audience research or when devising an audience research project it is important to consider the underlying motives of those undertaking the research. We should ask some searching questions:

- Who is conducting this research and why? (Is this research motivated by commercial imperatives, moral concerns, civic responsibility or curiosity?)
- Who is being researched and why?
- What questions are being asked and how are they being interpreted?

---

[4]http://press.uchicago.edu/ucp/books/book/distributed/F/bo26237077.html

- What methodologies are being used and are these appropriate to the task?

And perhaps even more importantly,

- How is the audience being 'constructed'?

In many, if not most, instances of media audience research, the audience is a function of the design of the researcher's project. People as individuals are 'assembled' as an audience for the purpose of the study. The audience, in other words, is an imagined construct.

These are the questions and the issues we need to keep in the back of our mind as we consider what we can learn from the history of media audience research, even as we try to come to terms with the rapidly evolving media landscape. At which point it might be worth bearing in mind that while media technologies change what motivates people to turn to the media and the values that they derive from their audiencing practices may be much more constant than is generally assumed – as Chapter 3, on the history of media technologies and media audience research, will suggest.

3 Technologies of Audiencing

The ways in which media audiences have been imagined in relation to different media technologies has much to do with ongoing debates about the psychological, physical, social, political and inevitably moral implications of the media form in question for those who use them in the practice of audiencing. While these debates begin with book and other forms of printed material, they gather momentum with the birth of the film industry at the turn of the 20th century, at a moment when sociology and social psychology as disciplines are seeking to establish themselves as a legitimate sciences in the academy. While concern about what audiences 'read' may have shifted from the book, the newspaper, the comic and the magazine to the kinds of content people can access on their personal digital device, when it comes to what people *hear* rather than *see* there is rather less audience research to draw on. This is despite the fact that according to a recent Nielsen (2018) report, an American adult listens to an average of 1.46 hours of radio per day. According to this survey, of all the available media platforms in the home it is radio that has the highest reach (92 per cent) across the population. With the current global popularity of podcasting, it would appear that the time is more than ripe for a reinvestigation of the role of radio in the current media landscape.

Underlying many of the debates that have swirled around the introduction of each emergent media technology is the issue of 'technological determinism'. The proposition that technology may shape society and its cultural values can be traced back to Karl Marx and his critique of the forces shaping labour relations and economic power during the industrial revolution in the 19th century. As Allan Dafoe (2015, p. 1048) has more recently argued, central to the issue of technological determinism is the question of agency and the degree of control that people have over the technology that they use. As Dafoe suggests, while those who assume a 'macro' perspective, regarding the larger social patterns of history through a long lens, tend to affirm the ways in which technology may produce social change, those who adopt a more 'micro' perspective, involving detailed, smaller-scale studies, are more likely to assert the agency of those affected. As Dafoe concludes, it is just possible that both perspectives have validity and there is a need to find a balance between the two (2015, p. 1058). Writing about the introduction of new media technologies, Nancy Baym has more faith in human agency. While she agrees that media technologies and platforms may have affordances that can push people in some directions rather than others, nevertheless people have the power to shape the contexts, the uses and the consequences of the technologies they use (Baym, 2015, p. 179). As this chapter will reveal, there have been a number of significant studies in the history of media audience research that have set out to explore what happens when a new media technology is introduced and the implications this may have for people's lives.

The written word

Before there were books, there were manuscripts, and before that other forms of writing on a variety of surfaces for the purposes of communication, including hieroglyphics, cuneiform texts and runic inscriptions. The writing of a manuscript, however, which designates a script written by hand, involved the production of a text that could be read by only the privileged few who were themselves able to read. One famous example sitting on the shelf of my study is a handsome reproduction of the illuminated manuscript known as *The Book of Kells*, produced by anonymous monks in Ireland sometime around the 8th or 9th centuries, nobody is quite sure when. Just to add to the confusion, there appears to be no single author of this text, nor was it all produced in one place. The monks who laboured over this magnificent book were simply making a copy of the four gospels to be found in New Testament translated into Latin. *The Book of Kells* was the product of many collective minds and hands.

What makes this the book unique, however, was not the content of the text but the elaborate illustrations combining Christian iconography, motifs drawn from Celtic art as well as the inventive and cartoonish designs woven into the script that appear to have been put there not just as an act of devotion, but also for the aesthetic appreciation, enjoyment or even the amusement of the creators and/or the readers of the text as is evident in the image below. 'Fun' might even have been involved. The art of this manuscript therefore tells another story or set of stories altogether about the people that created it:

Illustration 3.1 An illuminated page from the Gospel of St Matthew from *the Book of Kells*
Credit: Ancient Art and Architecture/Alamy Stock Photo.

When it comes to who might have seen this text, we know very little about its readership. During the 8th century there would have been very few people apart from the monks themselves who would have been able to read and understand a manuscript written in Latin, should they have been allowed to view it. This book was therefore a sacred object, not least because of the fact that it was unintelligible to all but the privileged few.

Fast forward to Germany in 1439, and Jonas Gutenberg is credited with the invention of the printing press in the Western world that made it possible to produce multiple copies of the same text in the languages people themselves were speaking at the time. In combination with growing rates of literacy, the potential readership for a book thus became bigger and many more books were produced. It is at this point that it became possible for people to read a religious text like the Bible for themselves, to take it home even, especially if this were translated into their own language. This scenario subsequently created much anxiety amongst the leaders of the religious establishment during the period known as the Reformation. If people were able to read the Bible in their own language and think about what they had read, rather than having a representative of the church read and interpret the text for them in Latin, then the power of the church itself might also be undermined. And so it came to pass.

The notion of power, who has it and who doesn't, has continued to be critical within the history of media audience research, not just in terms of content but also in terms of who controls access to that content, especially when it disappears into the private space of the home. In some instances, this has led to various forms of censorship, particularly in the vexed areas of screen violence and pornography (Barker and Petley, 1998; Williams, 1999; Sullivan and McKee, 2015). As is clearly evident in this history, some content is considered more dangerous than others. In the case of a religious text such as the Bible, translated from the Latin into a vernacular that people could understand and reproduced on a printing press that enabled copies to be circulated within a literate society, we have the perceived power inherent in a text that gives people access to the written word independently of those who have traditionally had control over this information. In this instance, those in power clearly imagined the media audience as potentially 'active', even 'subversive', readers, able to interpret and act on what they might read. While the concept of the 'active audience' is one that is associated with later development in media audience research, and was much championed by media scholars such as John Fiske (1989a, 1989b) and Henry Jenkins (1992), it is worth noting that the notion of the active audience existed as a possibility at a much earlier stage in thinking about media audiences.

The rise of the modern novel in the 18th century was also significant because it is at this point that we encounter some insights into a different, although by now rather familiar, construction of the audience. In this case we are talking about the imagined readers of the popular gothic novel: an enthralling genre of fiction featuring damsels in distress, haunted castles and evil villains. While the origins of the gothic novel are often traced back to *The Castle of Otranto* (1764), written by Englishman Horace Hugh Walpole, 30 years later it was another gothic novel, *The Mysteries of Udolpho*, that was a runaway bestseller. Written by Ann Radcliffe and originally published in three volumes in 1794, *Udolpho* went into a number of reprints, which, although small by today's standards, at the time would have raised the book to 'blockbuster' status. Even more significant is the fact that the popularity of the gothic novel inspired another author, Jane Austen, to write a famous parody entitled *Northanger Abbey*, which was not published until after her death in 1817, although it was originally written between 1798 and 1799.

In *Northanger Abbey*, the young and impressionable Catherine Moreland is so excited by her reading of gothic novels that this might be considered to have 'causal effect' on the ways in which she responds to people and events in the real world, with disastrous, funny, but hardly fatal, consequences. This is after all a comic satire. *Northanger Abbey* is nevertheless a telling construction of the ways in which the supposedly young and innocent *female* readership for the gothic novel is imagined as an impressionable and vulnerable, not to mention silly, audience. As Andreas Huyssen (1986) has effectively argued, the feminization of the mass audience for popular culture began with the readership for the novel in the 19th century and continues into the 20th in relation to new media forms and technologies. Ironically, similar anxieties about the susceptible female consumer of popular culture were to resurface during the early stages of the second wave of feminism in relation to contemporary genres such as magazines for girls (McRobbie and McCabe, 1981), TV soap operas (Modleski, 1982) and romance novels (Radway, 1984), although these genres were subsequently reclaimed and re-evaluated in a more positive light (Brown, 1994).

Moving pictures

In considering the long history of media audience research devoted to the film, it is salutary to consider one of the founding myths of film spectatorship since this helps to establish a set of anxieties, and myths, that have continued to recur in relation to all new media technologies, but especially those that involve an image on a screen. In 1896, the Lumière brothers in Paris, who had been experimenting with the medium of film, showed one of their first documentary short films. This portrayed the rather banal event of a train pulling into a station and the passengers alighting onto the platform (*L'Arrivée d'un train en gare à la Ciotât*). According to the myth, which is given shape and form in a vivid scene in the film *Hugo* directed by Martin Scorsese (2012), the audience seated in front of the screen in the café where this film is being shown stand up in a panic and attempt to flee because the image of the oncoming train appears so 'real'. It might be noted that this was a silent film lasting only 50 seconds and would have been shown on a portable screen with the noise of the projector whirring as an accompaniment to the flickering image. Given that this screening was taking place in a café, it could be assumed that this was a social event and that people would have been well informed about what they were going to see in advance – a moving picture.

According to Martin Loiperdinger and Bernd Elzer (2004, p. 96), who have conducted an exhaustive investigation into the history of the Lumière films and their reception, contemporary reports that spectators panicked simply cannot be found. And yet, as Loiperdinger and Elzer argue, this legend of the hysterical and impressionable audience has become '*the* founding myth of the medium, testifying to the power of film over its spectators' (Loiperdinger and Elzer, 2004, p. 92). As further confirmation of this tendency to assume an impressionable audience, 20 years later in 1916 in the United States, Harvard psychology professor, Hugo Münsterberg published what was perceived to be a ground-breaking book entitled *The Photoplay: A Psychological Study*, in which he suggested that the intensity with which these 'plays', by which he meant films, might 'take hold' of their audiences must have some form of social effect and that the 'penetrating influence' of these 'moving pictures' was inevitably 'fraught with dangers' (Münsterberg cited in Jowett et al., 1996, p. 21). Even more worrying was the possibility that these films might become 'starting points for imitation and other motor responses' (Münsterberg cited in Jowett et al., 1996, p. 21).

This observation reveals not only that film was already being considered in terms of its psychological effects, but also that within 20 years film viewing had gone from being a novelty to a becoming an established part of American urban social life and experience. Indeed, so popular had the 'photoplays' become that the newly emergent film industry had attracted the attention of social scientists, educators, politicians, clergymen and social workers, all of whom perceived these productions, and the theatres in which they were shown, as a potential threat to the Protestant standards of morality and culture that they sought to impose on the community at large. What these conservative groups wanted was scientific proof of the negative effects of these encounters with the screen in order to gain control over the motion picture industry, with a view to censorship.

This desire for evidence of the harmful effects would eventuate in what has come to be known as the Payne Fund Studies. Published between 1933 and 1935, according to Jowett et al. (1996, p. 17), this 12-volume series of studies, initially entitled *Motion Pictures and Youth*, 'still constitutes one the most extensive evaluations ever undertaken of the role of the motion picture in American society'. Funded by the donors to a charitable organization (the National Committee for the Study of Juvenile Reading), that had as one of its goals the production of reading materials to promote citizenship, by 1927 this organization's interest had expanded to encompass the effects of the movies on young people. Led by a former pastor, William Harrison Short, the newly established National Committee for the Study of Social Values in Motion Pictures was established in New York. Short then set about recruiting qualified social scientists, educationalists and psychologists from universities across the country, whom he encouraged to find new and innovative ways of investigating this troubling phenomenon. According to Jowett et al., this study marks the beginning of large-scale mass communications research at a time when sociology was just beginning to emerge as a professionalized social science (Jowett et al., 1996, p. 2).

By the end of 1928, 14 different studies were planned encompassing a variety of research methods. These included 'scientific' laboratory-type tests involving a 'psychogalvanograph', a machine designed to pick up changes in a subject's heart rate when exposed to images on a screen ('The Emotional Responses of Children to the Motion Picture Situation'). Another study proposed to compare the movie-going autobiographies of middle-class college students with an existing collection of one thousand life histories collected from juvenile delinquents ('Movies, Delinquency and Crime') (Jowett et al., 1996, p. 89).

While the psychologists and social scientists involved in the study favoured 'scientific' approaches to collecting data that could be quantified, measured and analysed, it was clear that the sociologists favoured a 'behavioural approach'. They were, however, for the most part united in their goal. Chicago academic Herbert Blumer, who with graduate student Philip Hauser was responsible for the research involving motion picture autobiographies, was apparently opposed to the burgeoning movie industry and not above manipulating the evidence to reinforce his own opinions about the negative effects of these early encounters with the screen (Jowett et al., 1996, p. 78). Interestingly, Hauser's own master's thesis derived from the same research data came to a very different conclusion, suggesting that the movies generated 'mostly harmless and occasionally positive influences on the prisoner's behaviour' (Jowett et al., 1996, p. 79).

Cressey's study

The most compelling research of all in Jowett et al.'s detailed account of the trajectory of the Payne Fund project was the never completed or published study 'Boys, Movies and City Streets' by another Chicago trained sociologist, Paul G. Cressey, who fell ill during the project while also supporting a seriously ill wife. Despite the fact that this project did not see the light of day, Jowett et al. include both an incomplete first draft and a revised project proposal in their invaluable account. As a master's student Cressey had earlier conducted a controversial study of the then prevalent taxi-dance halls in Chicago where men would pay 10 cents to young women for a dance that might also involve a sexual encounter. Informed by what we would now describe as a mixed-method approach involving interviews with the dancers, the patrons and the owners, as well as an account of the function of these halls in an unsettled urban environment, this remarkable study, published in 1932 as *The Taxi-Dance Hall*, was reprinted as recently as 2008 and is still considered a landmark in the field.

Recruited to be part of the well-funded Payne Fund Studies by Chicago sociologist Frederic Thrasher, who also had an interest in juvenile delinquency, Cressey set about addressing the Reverend Short's brief of finding a causal link between the movies and problematic social behaviour. Except he didn't. This was largely a consequence of the comprehensive way in which Cressey set about the task, given that in his opinion, in order to understand the role of the cinema in the boys' lives, what was needed was an understanding of their total 'social situation' (Jowett et al., 1996, p. 126), what Pierre Bourdieu would later identity as their 'habitus' (Bourdieu, 1984). Cressey's methodological approach therefore once again encompassed a mixed-method approach, employing the kinds of ethnographic methods favoured by anthropologists. Apparently, Cressey had read the work of anthropologist Margaret Mead and understood the value of 'cultural transmission' (Jowett et al., 1996, p. 227).

After undertaking the preliminary research for this project, which was written up with Thrasher as a co-author in a draft report entitled 'The Community: A Social Setting for the Motion Picture', Cressey shifted his ground even further, after what Jowett et al. (1996, p. 217) describe as an 'epiphany'. In Cressey's opinion, the notion of causality on which both himself and the other Payne Fund researchers had been operating was too restrictive (Jowett et al., p. 217). Rather than asking how delinquent boys might be affected by the movies, Cressey determined that they needed to investigate the presence and function of the movie theatre on the city streets where the boys lived (Jowett et al., 1996, p. 219). In his chapter outline for a revised study entitled 'Boys, Movies and City Streets', submitted to the Payne Fund directors in 1934, Cressey therefore proposed an ambitious programme of research that would encompass a detailed description of what he described as the 'interstitial' East Harlem tenement district of Manhattan.

What Cressey proposed (based on his observations) was that a motion picture theatre constituted a 'social world' in and of itself. Not only were all 'movie houses' not the same in terms of the experiences they might offer, but what might go on in them could encompass an astonishing range of different activities from 'child birth to the auctioning of a vehicle' (Cressey as cited in Jowett et al., 1996, p. 223). Furthermore, while the theatres might constitute a 'sexual hunting ground' for those seeking heterosexual or homosexual encounters, they might also function as a place of escape from overcrowded apartments or as a place to keep warm and save on coal bills in winter. The social and practical functions of the movie theatres were therefore multiple and complex, even before Cressey got to the topic of how young people might relate to what they saw on the screen.

Cressey's main hypothesis, repeated over and over again in his detailed chapter outline, is that a boy's response to a 'photoplay' would inevitably be shaped by his social background, his emotional dynamics and his 'axiological' world (Cressey cited in Jowett et al., 1996, p. 225). For example, Cressey proposed to investigate the ways in which movies might provide a subject for conversation and how having seen the most recent movies might function as a form of social prestige, what today might be identified as 'cultural capital'. He also proposed the possibility that the cinema might constitute 'an incidental educational force', with young people seeking and finding knowledge that might be useful to them about fashion, mannerisms, etiquette, potential occupations and the solution to personal problems (Jowett et al., 1996, p. 233). The movie theatres, and the photoplays that were shown, were therefore of value to their audiences in multiple and complex ways.

In terms of the original task to fund a link between the movies and delinquency, Cressey was cautious, pointing to the characteristics of the specific social context first:

> With the ineffectiveness of the family, the school, and other institutions characteristic of the interstitial area, the possibility for

establishing within the individual mechanisms, habits and activities of an anti-social or proscribed nature needing only the stimulus of a photoplay 'to set them off' is presumably greater.

(Cressey cited in Jowett et al., 1996, p. 230)

Note the use of the word 'presumably' and 'possibility'. Cressey is suggesting that the influence of the movies is by no means a given. However, in a part of the city where legitimate employment was limited and crime was rife, figures like the underworld gangster, as represented in films like the popular *Little Caesar* (1931), might well appear attractive to those without hope or with an already problematic relationship with the law. Here Cressey once again insists that what the boys bring to the screen in terms of their own social and cultural experience will determine what they take from it.

Cressey's impressive and detailed outline for this project concludes with a set of recommendations that have become very familiar over the years in terms of the kinds of well-intended suggestions proposed by successive waves of researchers endeavouring to make media audience research instrumental in terms of implementing policy. These suggestions were, in fact, an addition made by the Reverend Short and members of the Payne Fund Board (Jowett et al., 1996, p. 236). What Cressey himself would have suggested we are unlikely to know. As it is, the recommendations advocate for the supervision of children in theatres, free ratings information, special family programmes at the weekend and the cultivation of study in schools 'in the field of motion picture appreciation and criticism' (Jowett et al., 1996, p. 236). Here the future discipline of film studies is imagined as a form of moral and critical gate-keeping, in much the same way that study of the popular media was proposed by English academics Frank R. Leavis and Denys Thompson in their book *Culture and Environment* in 1933.

Rethinking the cinematic spectator

As recent commentators on cinema history have noted (Maltby et al., 2011), the study of cinema and film as a discipline that emerged as an area of academic interest in the 1950s did not address the social experience of the movie goer. The French theorists who were at the forefront of cinema studies, such as André Bazin, who established the groundbreaking journal *Cahiers du Cinema* in 1951, were more concerned with what was on the screen and the construction of an imagined spectator in relation to this. The approach to film spectatorship that emerged in this burgeoning academic field during the 1970s thus tended to draw on psychoanalytic theories that equated the experience of watching a film in the dark with the subconscious state of dreaming. Drawing on the work of Sigmund Freud and Jacques Lacan, theories of film spectatorship were hardly concerned with real audiences at all.

Indeed, it is only relatively recently that a more sociological approach to the practice of cinema-going has emerged as a viable alternative. As Richard Maltby attests, there is now growing international interest in the circulation and consumption of films, with particular attention to the cinema 'as a site of social and cultural exchange' (Maltby, 2011, p. 3). This 'new cinema history' (Bowles, 2011) draws on historical geography, social history, economics and anthropology to look at how cinema-going practices relate to patterns of employment, urban development, transport systems and leisure practices (Maltby, 2011, pp. 9–10). This is an approach that insists that the experience of audiencing is not limited to the encounter with the screen but encompasses all the complex factors that it takes for that event to occur as well as what it might mean in social and cultural terms for those who participate, an approach that Cressey pioneered.

Considering the Payne Fund Studies as a whole and the two research traditions it represents – the one seeking empirical and 'scientific' evidence of the effects of the audience encounter with the media and the other employing a sociological and anthropological approach that looks at the context of the encounter and the kinds of practices involved – they have proceeded in an uneasy double step over the intervening years. At which point, I will fast forward to the arrival of television as a broadcast medium in the home in most advanced Western nations after the Second World War, as the medium that precipitated not only a whole new set of anxieties but a new wave of research about audience's exposure to images.

Television in the home

While cinema-going might have been an 'observable' behaviour to the extent that it happened for the most part in publicly accessible venues, watching television in the home was not. Like the consumption of the book, watching television was destined to become a private, domestic activity once families were able to afford the new technology as it became available after the Second World War. This inevitably exacerbated concerns about the possible effects of this medium in terms of the ways in which it might impact on the routines of family life. Once again, these concerns were focused on the impact of the new medium on children and how television might affect their social attitudes as well as their physical well-being. Such anxieties were the impetus for academic studies in a number of countries including the UK (Himmelweit et al., 1958) and the USA (Schramm et al., 1961), which set out to investigate the impact of the new medium at a critical moment in time.

In the UK, social psychologist Hilde Himmelweit from the London School of Economics and Political Science took the lead in a large-scale empirical study of the effect of television on the young (Himmelweit et al., 1958, p. v). Like the Payne Fund Studies, this was sponsored research, initiated in this case by the Audience Research Department of the British Broadcasting Corporation (the BBC) and supported by the charitable Nuffield Foundation. Clearly the BBC was hoping for a positive outcome in terms of their charter, which was, and still remains to this day, to 'inform, educate and entertain'.[1]

At the time when this research was conducted there were only 3 million television sets installed in the 15 million homes in the UK, but as Himmelweit noted there was already a 'good deal of concern' being expressed about the 'effect' of the new medium on children (Himmelweit et al., 1958, p. v). As outlined in the foreword to her report, this included the possibility that TV might cut into children's playtime outside, distract them from their homework or interfere with their attendance at youth clubs or games. One of Himmelweit's advantages in conducting this ambitious audience research project was therefore one of timing. Given the slow roll-out of the technology across the country, she was able to compare groups of children who had television in the home with those who did not. This enabled her to implement what might be described as a 'conventional experimental method', involving a comparison between those children who already had some experience of television with a control group who had not. For the comparisons to be valuable, however, each viewer had to be matched by a non-viewer who was as much like them as possible in terms of sex, age, intelligence and social background, and preferably in the same classroom (Himmelweit et al., 1958, p. 5).

---

[1] https://www.theguardian.com/media/2014/jul/01/bbc-inform-educate-entertain-order

In the main study, four and a half thousand children were surveyed in London, Portsmouth, Sunderland and Bristol. In another, over children in Norwich were contacted both before and after the arrival of television in their area. In each case, the research methods used included anonymous surveys, the use of personal diaries recording daily activities and questionnaires. The researchers thus claimed that they were able to take account of a child's personality, their behaviour, emotional reactions, tastes, reactions to violence, as well as their ability to learn and acquire information. There were also 11 so-called 'additional or 'special' studies that employed 'observational methods' and long, informal interviews with individuals and groups, resulting in a variety of 'qualitative data'. This included a study in which 9–10-year-olds were interviewed about the role that television played in their lives, and another with special reference to their reactions to Westerns and crime and detective series on television (Himmelweit et al., 1958, p. 9).

According to Himmelweit's findings, the key factor determining how children watched television was 'intelligence': the brighter the child, the less television watched (Himmelweit et al., 1958, p. 12). Furthermore, 'the popular image of the child glued to the television set' did not fit the facts. While Himmelweit and her colleagues found that children in television households were slightly more likely to stay indoors and to share both their time and leisure activities with their parents, for the most part television appeared to displace other activities that children considered to be the equivalent of watching television, like going to the movies. This was not good news for the film industry, although according to Himmelweit et al. it appeared that during adolescence television became less important as young people preferred to leave the family home and go to the cinema as the preferred social option.

As Sonia Livingstone has noted, this study was integral to framing the new field of media research both in Britain and elsewhere (Livingstone, 2002, p. 24). It was however, very much of its time. As Livingstone points out, the questions posed were relatively simple and indeed testable; that is, what happens when one significant change is made to children's lives, 'namely the introduction of one national, terrestrial, public service television channel' (Livingstone, 2002, p. 24). Incidentally, this study therefore reveals a great deal about the cultural context of the 1950s in Britain, family life and the then current role of the media in society. Like the unpublished Cressey study, it thus provides a fascinating glimpse into the complexity of the lives of those involved at a specific historical moment.

In the USA, Wilbur Schramm, Jack Lyle and Edwin B. Parker from Stanford University in California were sufficiently inspired by Himmelweit's research to conduct their own study in the United States and Canada. They began by considering the use of television by children in the first six grades of the San Francisco school system. However, as a result of an injection of funds from the National Educational Television and Radio Center, this research was extended to include a study of 12th graders in their final year of high school in five Rocky Mountain communities, as well as two communities in Canada that had not as yet had exposure to TV (Schramm et al., 1961, p. v). In total, 11 different research studies were conducted as part of this project over a time frame of two years from 1958 to 1960. The various methods used included interviews with the children, their families and their teachers, questionnaires and classroom tests and the use of viewing diaries. The resulting publication, *Television in the Lives of Our Children*, comprises eight chapters that describe the findings in general terms. The data on which these conclusions are drawn are included in the 11 detailed appendices, including 97 pages of tables and statistics.

The outcomes of this wide-ranging study, which was expected to provide the US Congress with evidence about the negative effects of television on children, have since become legendary in the history of media audience research for their non-committal and cautiously italicized wording:

> For *some* children, under *some* conditions, *some* television is harmful. For *other* children under the same conditions, or for the same children under *other* conditions, it may be beneficial. For *most* children, under *most* conditions, *most* television is probably neither particularly harmful nor particularly beneficial.
>
> (Schramm et al., 1961, p. 1)

In other words, as Cressey had already determined in his unpublished study of the boys in East Harlem and their encounters with the screen, it all depends. Perhaps what is most interesting about Schramm's study is that it rejected the notion that children were the passive victims of an active television monster. Nothing could be further from the fact, Schramm et al. insisted, pointing out that it is children who are active in this relationship with the medium: 'It is they that use television, rather than television that uses them' (Schramm et al., 1961,

p. 1). This is an argument that denies the logic of technological determinism, while failing to account for the larger changes that the introduction of television might have had on family life or even domestic architecture.

Television and family life

Despite Schramm et al.'s attempts to allay social fears about television, these anxieties continued as the technology developed throughout the second half of the 20th century. *The* Plug-In *Drug: Television, Children and the Family* by Marie Winn, first published in 1977, proved to be both popular and influential in fuelling the conservative attacks on the medium. In 2002, a 25th anniversary edition was published, with the new subtitle *Television, Computers, and Family Life*, in which Winn extended her critique to the Internet and the worldwide web. Central to Winn's concerns about the role of television and computers are once again the ways in which these technologies are presumed to have a negative impact on family life. However, while Winn's account might be described as a 'macro' account that deals with the imagined 'big picture', as Dafoe suggested, a more 'micro' approach tends to produce a rather different impression.

In 1986 David Morley conducted a study of television in the family described by Stuart Hall in his introduction as a 'seminal piece of research into the social uses of television' (Hall, 1986, p. 7). Who, Morley asked, got to make the choices about what to watch and when and how could this be understood 'in the overall context of family life?' (1986, p. 13). The project encompassed interviews with 18 families living in South London in their own homes during the spring of 1985. All of the families possessed a video recorder; all were white and all comprised two adults living together with two or more dependent children. While initially the two parents were interviewed alone, later in the interview their children were invited to take part in the discussion along with their parents (Morley, 1986, p. 51). For anyone familiar with the interview as a research method, the conduct of these interviews begs a number of questions. For example, what difference would it have made to the findings if the members of these families had been interviewed separately, especially since what emerged from Morley's studies was the nature of the power and gender relations in the home and how these impacted on viewing practices. Nevertheless, Morley's research provides some valuable insights into the domestic economy and power relations in the household and how these may have impacted on the experience of watching television and using the video recorder.

According to Morley, in the majority of the homes where the father was 'the breadwinner' it was he who (apparently) controlled the television and the use of the video recorder as well as the choice of programmes. This was symbolized by jealous guardianship of the remote control. The only exception to this rule was in those households where the father was unemployed and the mother was working (1986, p. 149). What was also revealing about this research were the ways in which programme type preferences were differentiated along gender lines. While men 'said' they preferred news and current affairs, women preferred drama, while the watching of daytime soaps was characterized as a guilty secret, thus signifying the women's appreciation of the perceived low status of their chosen genre.

Other significant differences identified by Morley included gender-based viewing styles – men reported that they tended to watch with concentration while women said they watched in a distracted way while doing something else, usually a domestic chore. The inference Morley draws from these claims is that while for the male breadwinners the home might be a site of leisure, for women it is always the site of the domestic labour. Nor would the situation with regards to domestic labour appear to have changed much since. In Australia, the 2016 census data revealed that while women spent between five and fourteen hours a week doing unpaid domestic housework, for men it continues to be less than five hours.[2] The relationship between family viewing and domestic labour was also central to Ann Gray's 1994 study of the video recorder that included the revelation that women tended to be averse to learning how to programme the family video recorder lest this become yet another domestic chore they were required to perform. Women's professed incompetence when it came to programming and operating the video recorder was therefore strategic rather than innate.

Although the allocation of domestic work in the home may not have changed so much, with women still bearing the brunt of this, during the 1990s the media landscape in the home was changing. According to Livingstone, the family home in an advanced Western

---

[2] https://theconversation.com/census-2016-women-are-still-disadvantaged-by-the-amount-of-unpaid-housework-they-do-76008

economy was undergoing a transformation 'into a site of a multimedia culture' that included the use of computers, personalized mobile phones and digital television (Livingstone, 2002, p. 1). In the face of these developments, while according to Livingstone there were, as always, the 'optimists', foreseeing new opportunities for democratic and community participation, creativity, self-expression and play, there were also the 'pessimists', lamenting the ways in which these media technologies might lead to 'the end of childhood, innocence, traditional values and authority' (Livingstone, 2002, p. 2). Central to this latest set of anxieties was access to the Internet and the potential impact of encountering violent, stereotypical, commercially exploitative or pornographic content (Livingstone, 2002, p. 5). As Livingstone notes, these are concerns that echo those expressed about the arrival of every other new media form including the VCR, the introduction of television and film – as well as radio and comic books (Livingstone, 2002, p. 5). Despite the 'flurry of hype and anxiety', she argues, there lies a 'dearth of knowledge about the social meanings, uses and consequences of new information technologies', a 'dearth' that clearly necessitated a new enquiry into the role of the media in children's lives.

'New' media

Livingstone's explicit intention in her subsequent study, originally entitled *Young People New Media*, was to update Himmelweit et al.'s (1958) findings by charting the current access and use of 'new media' in the home. This included an investigation of domestic leisure and media activities in order to shed light on the ways in which families were adapting to a changing media environment (Livingstone, 2002, p. 252). The study also entailed a cross-national component, with parallel studies conducted in 12 different European countries, each research team following a common conceptual framework and methodology, incorporating both qualitative and quantitative methods including large-scale surveys involving 'some 15,000 children and young people aged 6–16' (Livingstone, 2002, p. 252).

In Livingstone's discussion of the key findings, four key themes are identified. (Livingstone, 2002, pp. 18–19). While the first is the multiplication of personally owned media, leading to the conclusion that the notion of 'family television' as espoused by David Morley (1986) was rapidly becoming obsolete, the second points to the ways in which the diversification of the media in terms of both form and content has led to much greater flexibility in the ways in which people organize their individual media preferences. The third theme to emerge relates media convergence to a blurring of the lines between the traditional boundaries between home/work, entertainment/information, education/leisure, masculine/feminine. The fourth major change, which Livingstone (2002, p. 20) suggests is the most radical of all, is the shift from 'one way, mass communication towards more interactive communication between medium and user'.

In making these observations, Livingstone is careful to avoid both technological and cultural determinism by paying attention to the complexity of political, social and economic forces that have also shaped family life since the Second World War when television first entered the home. The 1950s, she argues, was 'a golden era in the public image of family life', when the ideal of the affluent suburban nuclear family with its consumer lifestyle comprising a breadwinner father, a housewife mother and their two children were also reflected on the screen. The reality, she notes, has always been somewhat different, as Himmelweit's research also revealed (Livingstone, 2002, p. 23). Children in the 1950s stayed up late, watched programmes that were unsuitable for them and – as someone who lived through that period in the UK can attest – might choose *not* to watch television with their parents, preferring to express their individuation by reading. The image of a cosy family basking in the glow of the electronic hearth may well have been a chimera for many.

As Livingstone suggests, claims that the signs of individualization apparent in the 1990s media landscape could be signalling the end of family television and family togetherness were probably wrong on both accounts: the ideal of the traditional nuclear family in all its togetherness may never have existed then and the individuation that is believed to be occurring in the present may be far less dramatic than imagined. Hence the need for empirical research, which brings us to the advantages of participant observation rather than other forms of self-reporting and the possibilities that user-generated material on the Internet might afford when it comes to doing audience research into how people use the media in the home.

How families 'really' watch media

One of the most interesting 'genres' of user-produced content to arrive on YouTube are video clips that record people watching TV in real time. Setting aside for the moment the ethical problems relating to privacy and consent that would be unlikely to get past a university research committee, a quick search under the category 'people watching television' produced a video clip of an Australian family 'watching' a football Grand Final (Australian Rules) in 2011. This piece of 'found' visual anthropology (which has subsequently been taken down from YouTube) beautifully illustrated the complex choreography of media use in a family living room using time lapse.[3] It also, incidentally, recalls Herman Bausinger's account of Mr Meier's weekend trying to watch a football match on television. However, while Bausinger was able to offer us an account of the motivations underlying the (fictional?) Mr Meier's viewing strategies, here the random viewer is left adrift to work this out for themselves.

While it is evident that we are dealing with some kind of ritual here – the viewing of the Football Grand Final that is also an excuse for a social family gathering – what this clip cannot reveal, of course, is what is going on people's heads as they experience this moment in time, the precise nature of the relationships involved and just how the media experience, to which they are only intermittently attending, might matter to them. In order to discover this, we would have to ask every member of the family, although this might not be as useful as we would hope given that accounting for one's media practices also involves a degree of face-saving. Even supposing the members of this family were willing or able to explain the complexity of their social viewing experience, we would probably find that each of their responses differed in some critical way.

In terms of what we can see in this clip, our viewpoint is that of the camera located in a corner of the room, above and slightly behind the television screen. The field of vision includes a couch and an armchair in front of the TV, there are upright dining chairs facing the screen at the rear of the room. The door is open and there is a useful clock on the wall revealing that the chronology of the action is from around 2.30 in the afternoon to about 5 pm, although the length of the clip is a scant 1.45 minutes. There are initially eight people watching the television, encompassing what appear to be three couples. One set (grandparents?) are older than the other two and there are two small girls who appear to be in the 8–10 age range. Another younger couple arrives

---

[3]Sadly it would appear that a request to use images from this clip which the producer declined may have precipitated its removal from YouTube. Nevertheless, as a form of vernacular audience research, it was extremely effective.

midway through the afternoon's viewing and are present intermittently for the rest of the time.

Although we are completely in the dark about who these people might be and where they are, what this footage illustrates is that while the ritual of watching a sporting match may be the excuse to bring what appears to be an extended family together, they are constantly on the move over the two and a half hours. A range of food is consumed, including at one point a birthday cake, while beer bottles and cans mount up on the table. People change their position, leave and re-enter the room, talk to different people, cuddle and embrace. After about an hour the two little girls occupy one of the easy chairs and proceed to devote themselves to a shared tablet computer. At one point no one appears to be watching the TV at all.

Towards the end of the game, a couple sit side by side on the couch looking at their separate mobile phones. They are together apart in ways that beautifully illustrate the oxymoron that is at the heart of the contemporary media experience, although unlike Sherry Turkle in her book *Alone Together* (2011), I do not consider this to be necessarily a negative one. Nevertheless, concern that technological change may lead to a loss of sociability and the erosion of family life has become a key concern underpinning contemporary audience research.

The networked home

When it comes to how internet connectivity and a converged media landscape have impacted family life, there are, as always, many other factors to consider, as Melissa Gregg vividly illustrates in her book *Work's Intimacy* (2011). Gregg's findings are the outcome of a postdoctoral research project conducted between 2007 and 2009, entitled 'Working from Home: New Media Technology, Workplace Culture and the Changing Nature of Domesticity'. Here Gregg explores the ways in which internet connectivity has contributed to a blurring of the boundaries between home and work. Over the course of three years, Gregg interviewed 26 people working in four different organizational settings (education, government, broadcasting and telecommunications), in order to determine how they were managing technology in relation to their work practices. At the start of this period, Brisbane was experiencing something of a boom time that inevitably impacted all those involved. Gregg is therefore careful to situate her participants' experiences in relation to the evolving political, social and cultural context, which included the commercial release of the iPhone in Australia in 2009.

Gregg is cautious not to overstate the case, suggesting that the rapid embrace of new media technology in order to stay in touch and work from home merely exacerbates what was in fact 'a much older tendency among salaried professionals to put work at the heart of daily concerns' (Gregg, 2011, p. xi). As a result, 'work has now broken out of the office, downstairs to the café, in to the street, on to the train, and later still to the living room, dining room, and bedroom' (Gregg, 2011, p. 1). Online connectivity, Gregg suggests, has thus served to consummate a pre-existing middle-class infatuation with work (Gregg, 2011, p. xi) while having potentially negative effects on the lives of the working women involved. Not only do they now do all of the cooking and cleaning, but also have to wait until the rest of the house is asleep in order to have time to work alone at home (Gregg, 2011, p. 3).

Gregg's account is vividly illustrated by the experiences of her participants, many of whom seem unaware of the extent to which work has crept into their leisure time. As such, 'checking email was the work that dare not identify itself as such' (Gregg, 2011, p. 46). This leads Gregg to the conclusion that the ways in which people have embraced new media technologies in order to stay in touch with work accords well with a neoliberal form of governance that ensures workers perceive their work activities at home as a form of personal freedom (Gregg, 2011, p. 3). As Gregg points out, there is a problem here in that there are no formal policies governing the management of work email in terms of minimum response times or even expectations regarding time limits. As Gregg argues, a key platform of Labor politics in Australia and socialist policies in general has always rested on the notion that there should be limits to the working day (Gregg, 2011, p. 14). None of these issues is insoluble. As Gregg argues, her research suggests that there is a real need for organizations to take greater responsibility in redefining workloads and work practices at the same time as workers also need to take responsibility to push back against 'the symptoms of professional presence bleed' (Gregg, 2011, p. 169). The use of online technologies can be managed.

Audiencing in practice

While these observations about the use of new media technologies in the home might appear to take us away from the notion of 'audiencing' and further in the direction of the use of the media in everyday life, I would suggest that there are important connections to be made between the two. As a media academic, I would be the first to acknowledge that while I am sitting on the couch watching some form of screen entertainment, from the news and the weather report to the latest Netflix drama, I will also be checking my email regularly as I endeavour to keep ahead of my professional responsibilities. As Bausinger noted in 1984, long before the introduction of the internet-connected handheld digital device, the media are rarely used 'completely or with full concentration' (Bausinger, 1984, p. 47). As is evident from the YouTube clip described, even when gathered together for a significant media event such as a Football Grand Final there are many other factors that may be at work in the experience of being part of an audience. But how to capture these?

Although self-report mechanisms, surveys and a new 'cross-platform respondent-level data set' as employed by A. C. Nielsen (2018, p. 28) can provide us with data that tells us the percentage of people watching television, listening to the radio, using the Internet or apps on their smartphone or tablet as a share of daily time spent on each platform, it can tell us very little about how people are relating to the content they consume. As Chapter 4 will discuss, concern about what that content might be has also been a major driver of media audience research that has attempted to do just that, with varying degrees of success.

4 Content and Interpretation

One of the key drivers of media audience research has been a concern about the types of media content that people choose to consume and the effects that this may have on their thinking and/or behaviour. As a consequence, there is a considerable continuity in the kinds of content that have inspired related audience research projects over the course of the 19th and 20th centuries and the new millennium as media technologies and platforms have evolved, diversified and fragmented. While this concern might have begun with questions of taste and the emergence of working-class literacy, it has included political debates about the ideological messages embedded in media content as well as moral concerns about the impact of sex, violence and consumerism – from the lurid 19th-century broadsheets and peepshows to the practice of sending images online known as 'sexting'. While the latter may be intended for an audience of a few, the anxiety about these images as a form of media arises when the audience is presumed to be many.

Other specific types of content that have attracted the attention of researchers and have resulted in significant research studies would include media forms such as the gangster film (Blumer, 1933), radio soap opera (Herzog, 1944), the comic book (Wertham, 1954), women's magazines (Hermes, 1995; Winship, 1987), television soap operas (Modleski, 1982; Ang, 1985; Liebes and Katz, 1993; Brown, 1994), romance fiction (Radway, 1984), 'video nasties' (Barker, 1984), reality TV (Mathijs and Jones, 2004; Hill, 2005) and speculative fiction and/or fantasy on screen (Jenkins, 1992; Bacon-Smith, 1992). Indeed, the popularity of the American TV series *Star Trek* clearly contributed to the emergence of a specific off-shoot of media audience research, now referred to as fan studies, following the publication of Henry Jenkins' ground-breaking book, *Textual Poachers* in 1992, not forgetting Camille Bacon-Smith's *Enterprising Women* published in the same year. There is now also a considerable body of significant audience research devoted to cult media texts such as *Dr Who, The Lord of the Rings, The Hobbit,*

Harry Potter and *Game of Thrones* to name only a few, that has attempted to explore the global popularity of these multiplatform media phenomena as they have extended their reach and impact across time and across space.

While much media content can now be accessed online, since the turn of the millennium the emergence of media platforms such as Facebook, YouTube and Instagram have made it possible for people to create and share their own content. This is content that is accessible to anyone, anywhere and anytime with the appropriate technology and the statistics are mind-boggling. Since the first YouTube video 'Me at the Zoo' was uploaded on 23 April 2005 by former PayPal employees Chad Hurley and Steve Chen, depicting their colleague Jawed Karim standing awkwardly in front of an enclosure at the zoo, pointing out the existence of the elephant's trunk, YouTube has evolved from a relatively unambitious video-sharing site into what Burgess and Green (2018, p. 1) describe as a mainstream media platform with a complex relationship to broadcast and cable television, not forgetting the music business. The platform now hosts over a million home-grown YouTube stars producing a diverse range of content that attracts billions of subscribers. From video blogs or 'vlogs' (in which people address the camera in a face-to-face confessional) to 'un-boxing' videos (that focus on the pleasure to be derived from unpacking consumer goods), new forms of content are attracting large audiences that call for new types of investigation to discover how and why this type of content matters.

The effects paradigm

The assumption of influence, that media content can directly affect the ways in which people think and behave, depends on the notion of causality. That is, that one thing (a media message) causes another thing (a reaction) to happen in much the same way that lighting a flame under a pot of water will cause the water to boil. In this formulation of a media effect, people are assumed to respond to the messages embedded in the content to which they are exposed in terms of both their thinking and/or behaviour. In fact, how people respond to the media content they consume is by no means a given. While the history of media audiences is haunted by the notion of an undifferentiated 'mass' audience imagined as passive and susceptible to whatever message is embedded in the media content they consume, this assumes that everyone receives that content in exactly the same way. However, people are not the same and how they interpret and respond to any form of content will to a large extent depend on the knowledge, experience and capabilities they bring to the task.

In order to illustrate this, think about a time when you and someone else (a friend or a member of your family) have read the same book, watched the same TV show or film or viewed the same content online, and have had quite different reactions to it. You may have differed in terms of whether you liked or disliked it, what you thought was interesting or uninteresting, good or bad, funny or unfunny or what it even 'meant'. It may also have 'affected' you quite differently, both intellectually and emotionally. Note the distinction between the word 'affect' rather than 'effect', two words that are often confused in media audience research. In choosing to use 'affect' here, I am pointing to the possibility that media content may touch your feelings or 'move' you in some emotional way. An 'effect' on the other hand, can be anything which changes or is altered as a result of that experience.

The *Oxford Dictionary* explanation is intended to be helpful:

> Affect is chiefly used as a verb, and its main meaning is 'to influence or make a difference to' … Effect on the other hand, is used as both a noun and a verb, although it most commonly used as a noun. As a noun it means 'a result or influence'.[1]

Putting these two terms into practice might be more helpful in illuminating their subtle difference. For example, watching with my adult son the much lauded battle scene frequently referred to as 'The Battle of the Bastards' (season 6, episode 9), in the cult American TV series *Game of Thrones* (HBO 2011–19) on first release on the pay platform Foxtel in Australia, I spent a great deal of the time with my eyes covered. While I was strongly *affected* by the bloodshed and violence, my son delighted in what he assured me were the computer-generated imagery (CGI) special *effects*. What *affected* me most was the apparent damage done to the horses involved, while this had no *effect* on my son at all, because he was able to 'discount' this violence as 'not real'. In *effect*, while together we might have agreed about what the text represented in very broad terms, and how *effective* it was, we had very different responses to it; responses that depended on our prior knowledge that inevitably *affected* our interpretation and hence our reactions.

---

[1] https://en.oxforddictionaries.com/usage/affect-or-effect

There have been many attempts to account for what is happening when people make sense of a text, whether this be in a written text or a more graphic form. In the sections that follow, I shall outline two of these in very broad terms. While the first these involves the science of semiotics and the study of 'signs', another involves what has variously been described as 'reader-response theory' and/or 'reception theory'.

A question of interpretation

Semiotics has two points of origin in the 19th century: the work of American philosopher Charles Sanders Peirce and the work of Swiss-born linguist Ferdinand de Saussure. While there are similarities and differences in the approach to semiotics taken by these two thinkers, central to both is the concept of the sign and how this might be interpreted. To put it very simply, the word 'tree' as it is written on the page here has an entirely arbitrary relationship with what it represents, that is, a physical tree. As evidence of this, we might immediately point to the fact that different languages might have quite different linguistic 'signs' for a tree. In French it is 'arbre', while in an ideographic written language like Chinese the tree/wood radical (*zi pang*) would be written like this: 木.[2]

What semiotic theory suggests is that the arbitrary sign for a tree in any language (the signifier) points us to the concept of a tree in the real world (the signified). However, where this gets interesting is the possibility that your idea of a tree might well differ from mine. In other words, we might read the sign for a tree quite differently depending on our experience of trees in the past, the connotations that a tree has for us or how we think about trees in general. This becomes even more apparent when we consider another kind of sign for a tree altogether: the photograph of a tree. Before you read on, ask yourself what you see here (Illustration 4.1) and what it means to you.

Now consider the fact that this is a photograph of a tree in Iceland, a country where there are relatively few trees, a fact that is attributed not just to the sub-arctic, volcanic conditions and terrain, but also to history. It has been suggested that Iceland used to be covered with birch forests but that when the Vikings arrived in the 8th century, they

---

[2] The tree/wood 木 radical (*zi pang*) is seen in many Chinese characters that have an association with tree or wood. However, in simplified Chinese, the general word for *tree* is written as 森 while *forest* is written as 森林 (a combination of five 木), representing the many trees in the forest.

Illustration 4.1 A lonely tree in Iceland
Credit: Cultura Creative (RF)/Alamy Stock Photo.

cut down all the trees in order to build houses and boats. Indeed, the Settlement Exhibition in downtown Reykjavik includes a diorama and commentary suggesting that this was indeed the case.[3] The larger point of this tree story, however, is to illustrate the possibility that how we interpret an image, in this case the photograph of a tree, may well depend on prior knowledge about trees that will inflect how we think about 'this' tree. The word 'tree' may therefore summon a very different set of connotations for an Icelander.

This example suggests that our interpretation of a complex sign like a photograph also depends on a set of prior knowledges and experiences. This proposition is at the heart of what, in literary theory, is described as 'reader-response theory'. Over the course of the 20th century, in a variety of different locations (in Europe and in the USA), literary scholars began to formulate a notion of the reader as an active interpreter of the text, and there are many academic books and articles that trace the often disputed origins and history of this concept. One of the more controversial versions of this thinking in the 20th century was to suggest that the text itself had no real existence until it was read. This led to French philosopher Roland Barthes (1967) famously declaring that the author was metaphorically 'dead', although the whole point of Barthes' provocative essay was to shift attention away from the intention of the author and towards the activity of the reader, whose

---

[3] http://borgarsogusafn.is/en/the-settlement-exhibition, accessed 24 July 2018.

interpretations of the text would depend on their own, unique, lived experience – no matter what the author may have originally intended.

In 1973, British academic and cultural studies theorist Stuart Hall effectively applied semiotics and reader-response theory to an understanding of how people make sense of a complex text like a television broadcast. In an essay entitled 'Encoding and Decoding in the Television Discourse', Hall begins by criticizing what he describes as 'linear' models of communication that assume an effective and simple transmission of content via a message sent from the producer to the consumer. In his formulation of this process, Hall points to the significance of the 'encoding' process – that is, all the choices that are made by the producer about the form that this television programme will take – and the equally important 'decoding' process – in which the receiver of the message (the television audience) will attempt to make sense of this.

In modelling this process, Hall was careful to point out that while audiences might well agree on what a particular programme might be about in general terms, what it might mean to them personally would come into play at the level of interpretation. Central to the process were the 'frameworks of knowledge' operational in both the production and reception of the broadcast. Implicit in Hall's 'frameworks of knowledge' is the concept of 'ideology', much debated in philosophical and sociological texts of the time. For example, French philosopher Louis Althusser famously defined ideology in 1971 as the 'representation of the imaginary relationship of individuals to their real conditions of existence'.[4] In other words, it is ideology that frames how we imagine the world to be and we may not even be aware of this until our thinking is challenged. A key example here might be the ongoing global debates about marriage equality in the new millennium that have questioned the assumption that the legal contract of a marriage should only be available to people of the opposite sex. Ideology is therefore a product of prior experience and social context, including such determinants as race, gender, class and education. In this way, ideology is operational in the production of any mediated form of communication, both in the 'encoding' process (the content created by the producers) as well as the 'decoding' process (how that content is received and interpreted by an audience).

In accounting for the process of encoding and decoding, Hall identified three possible audience positions in relation to the text in

---

[4] https://www.marxists.org/reference/archive/althusser/1970/ideology.htm, accessed 24 October 2017.

question: the 'dominant', the 'negotiated' and the 'oppositional'. According to Hall, a dominant reading would be one in which viewers accepted the ideological position inscribed in the text by the producers, a negotiated reading would employ some measure of critique, while an oppositional reading would reject the implicit ideology of the text and question the values that it represented. These concepts were subsequently tested by David Morley and Charlotte Brunsdon (1980) in a study of television audiences for a British current affairs show known as *The 'Nationwide' Audience*.

In this project, which marks a significant moment in the history of media audience research, a number of viewing groups were set up across the country. These audiences were constructed on the basis of their shared location, demographics and occupational status, with the presumption that they would also share the same ideological viewing positions. Each group was then shown the same episode of the current affairs programme, *Nationwide*, and their subsequent comments recorded and transcribed for analysis in order to determine the ways in which the participants positioned themselves in relation to the proposed dominant, negotiated or oppositional paradigms. Given the composition of these groups, it was hardly surprising that the findings tended to confirm expectations, although there were some occasional disagreements even within the like-minded groups (Morley and Brunsdon, 1980, p. 134).

One of the ongoing criticisms of the focus group methodology which this study employed is that groups who share a similar background and orientation are much more likely to reinforce each other's opinions. As a result, while the bank managers shared what was identified as the conservative and dominant reading of the text, it was hardly surprising (given their socialist politics) that the union organizers, the shop stewards, adopted an oppositional reading. The teacher training students, on the other hand, adopted a negotiated position, while the black further education students simply refused to engage with the content of the programme at all given that the content was by and large completely irrelevant to them (Morley and Brunsdon, 1980, p. 142). In this regard, it is interesting to speculate what might have occurred if Morley had mixed the groups up, putting people from different backgrounds into the various viewing groups, and whether this might have led to compromise or even more entrenched oppositional positions as a result of clashing ideologies. These are questions of methodology which will be discussed in more detail in Chapter 5.

Morley's research was subsequently criticized on the basis that the viewing groups constructed were artificial and that people would not normally watch a show like *Nationwide* together nor discuss it in this way. Morley acknowledged these criticisms, agreeing that these were not 'real audiences' and that this viewing experience was not how people would watch television in the course of their daily lives. Nevertheless, this study continues to figure as an important reference point in the history of media audience research because it represents an attempt to test a hypothesis about reading positions and the importance of 'ideology' and frameworks of knowledge to the ways in which people 'read' a text. In the context of the 2016 American presidential elections, the *Nationwide* research therefore took on a whole new relevance as it was argued that people, especially those on the extreme right wing of politics (alt-right) had consistently sought out news sources that confirmed rather than challenged their ideological positions and world view. Whether this was an effect of choice, or the algorithmic functions of Facebook that offers people 'more of the same' based on their prior choices, the fact that Facebook was implicit in the spreading of 'fake news' brings us to the issue of propaganda.

The anxiety of influence

In 2018 Facebook was accused of leaking data about its users to a range of different companies. One of these, the British company Cambridge Analytica was subsequently accused of harvesting the personal data from online sites affecting up to 87 million people worldwide, proving that far from it being a private listening or viewing space, the Internet is rather more public than people might imagine. This harvested data was then used to target potential voters, providing them with 'fake news' and other content that would inevitably shape their perception of specific events. These included the 2015 and 2016 election campaign of Donald Trump, the British vote to leave the European Union in 2016 (Brexit) and the Mexican general election in 2018.[5] As troubling as these revelations were, the concern about the power of the media to spread propaganda that this scandal raised were by no means new within the history of media audience research.

---

[5] Olivia Solon, 'Facebook says Cambridge Analytica may have gained 37m more users data', *The Guardian* online, 5 April 2018, https://www.theguardian.com/technology/2018/apr/04/facebook-cambridge-analytica-user-data-latest-more-than-thought, accessed 25 July 2018.

Indeed, a report published in 2014 by the Pew Centre for Independent Research in the United States entitled 'Political Polarization and Media Habits', with the telling subtitle 'From Fox News to Facebook, How Liberals and Conservatives Keep Up with Politics' (Mitchell and Weisel, 2014), revealed what was already common knowledge: that those on both the left and right wings of politics tend to choose news sources that confirm their ideological positions. Not only that, but those at the more extreme ends of the spectrum are more likely to act on their convictions in terms of voting, donating to campaigns and participating directly in politics (Mitchell and Weisel, 2014, p. 1).

Significantly, 47 per cent of those surveyed by the Pew Centre researchers who identified themselves as consistently belonging to alt-right groups were reliant on a single source of news, citing the American TV network owned by Richard Murdoch, Fox News, as their main source of information about government and politics (Mitchell and Weisel, 2014, p. 2). As a result of the algorithmic push and pull on Facebook, this ideologically inclined group were therefore more likely than others to come across political opinions that were in line with their own political views (Mitchell and Weisel, 2014, p. 2). While the authors were keen to stress that it is by and large impossible to live in an 'ideological bubble' and that those in the more extreme ideological positions are well aware of challenges to their views, it was also clear that any challenges did little to unsettle their positions. Indeed, it is argued that ideological positions were becoming more entrenched and even harder to shift as people turned to the news sources that continued to support and confirm them in their world view.

'We now live', according to journalist Roy Greenslade writing for the *Guardian* newspaper in 2016, 'in a post-truth society', a term that was very much in play in that year after both the US election and the earlier Brexit vote that saw the British public vote by a small margin to leave the European Union. However, as Greenslade was also keen to point out, while the propagation of false information on social media is not the fault of the platform itself, it is a consequence of the affordances of the platform that lies can be so easily spread (Greenslade, 2016), not forgetting the involvement of Cambridge Analytica. As people tried to make sense of Trump's win, attention inevitably turned to Facebook's use of algorithms, since someone who landed on a fake news site, or one hostile to Clinton and favourable to Trump, would be likely to be offered links to similar sites supporting the same views. The use of algorithms in news feeds is usefully explained by Lindsay Kolowich (2016) in a post to the marketing website HubSpot.

As Kolowich (2016) points out, when picking posts for those who log onto Facebook the algorithm has to take into account hundreds of variables on order to arrive at a 'relevancy score' based on your previous likes, clicks, comments, shares or rejections of a post as 'spam'. Once the potential posts to your site have been accorded a relevancy score, Facebook then ranks them in the order they will appear on your site. Not only are news posts accorded a relevancy score, but also the ads that appear with monotonous regularity as Facebook helps its advertisers find their target market.

Although the temptation to blame Facebook and other social media for the 2016 election outcome was therefore high, as Jason Mittell and Chuck Tryon (2016) have pointed out, America, like other countries in the Western world, has had a long history of right-wing media in print, radio and TV stretching back to the 1950s.

In this context, as Mittell and Tryon argue, it was the launch of media mogul Rupert Murdoch's Fox News in the mid-1990s that was the real game changer in the history of American journalism, given that from its very beginning Fox News broke with many of the standards embraced by traditional broadcast journalism. This included the introduction of personality-based commentary and the sensational 'click bait' news most likely to attract readers. Founded by Murdoch appointee Roger Ailes, Fox News also had close connections with the Republican Party. Indeed, following the departure of Ailes from Fox under a cloud of suspicion for his alleged sexual improprieties, Ailes went on to become Republican nominee Trump's adviser in the lead-up to the 2016 election. This was hardly a surprise, since, as Mittell and Tryon effectively argue, Fox News had always functioned as the propaganda arm for the right wing of politics. This suggestion was earlier revealed by the documentary film *Outfoxed* (2006) that demonstrated how the Fox News network was tightly controlled in terms of the editorial opinions that could be expressed and the 'experts' who might be consulted. Such policies included total support for the neoliberalist free-market economy and the denial of climate change.

While there were those who constantly drew attention to the bias of Fox News, including American satirist Stephen Colbert and the long-running animated sitcom *The Simpsons*, it would appear that such constant niggling did little to undermine the popularity or the credibility of the Fox News channel with its adherents. Ironically, the interventions of *The Simpsons* on the Fox network may have inadvertently served the purpose of suggesting that Fox News was willing to embrace its critics, the implication being that it had nothing to hide or fear.

The outcome of the 2016 election was, however, not entirely unforeseen. Also circulating on social media before the election were the predictions of Canadian philosopher Richard Rorty, who had suggested in 1998 before his death that 'something will crack'. In Rorty's opinion the non-suburban electorate would inevitably be looking around for a new 'strongman', someone who would assure them that the 'smug bureaucrats' and 'tricky lawyers', not forgetting the 'postmodernist professors', should no longer be in power. Even more prescient, Rorty predicted that all the gains made over the last 40 years in race, sexual and gender politics would be erased as those who considered themselves to have been discriminated against would express their rage against a system that appeared not to take their views into account. In other words, Rorty predicted the rise of Trump and the deep rifts that have since emerged in American society and politics.

In terms of audience research, it would therefore appear that the survey methods employed by the US pollsters prior to the election constituted a very blunt instrument when it came to finding out how people were actually thinking about the future and Donald Trump. Indeed, as was evident from the many vox pops that appeared on television in the run-up to the election, ordinary people from all walks of life were 'reading' Trump in terms of their own desires for a 'strongman'. At which point we might return to the science of semiotics in order to speculate on how Republican nominee Donald Trump was used as a 'sign' by those on the left of this divide. One of the more compelling ways in which Donald Trump was signified can be found in an ongoing series of cover images for the magazine the *New Yorker* that often used only his elaborate comb-over to stand for the man himself. Openly hostile to Trump, the magazine continued to critique the man and the presidency both before and after his election in 2016.

In February 2017, two weeks into Trump's presidency, the magazine featured a cover image showing five previous presidents of the United States (John F. Kennedy, Abraham Lincoln, Theodore Roosevelt, George Washington and Harry S. Truman) watching Trump on television, their faces expressing a range of expressions from disapproval to horror (see Illustration 4.2). The interpretation of this image, however, requires at least some knowledge of American history as well Trump's own use of the media, including his stint on the reality show *The Apprentice*, in order to appreciate exactly how the magazine was positioning Trump as the object of disapproval.

In thinking about the interpretation of media texts, it is therefore evident that people can only make sense of this content with reference

Illustration 4.2 Cover illustration, Barry Blitt, The New Yorker, February 1, 2016. © Condé Nast

to the frameworks of knowledge that they bring to the task. Furthermore, any interpretation will inevitably draw on previous experience, including encounters with similar media texts, and the viewer's own political orientations, however these have been formed.

While the *New Yorker* cover espouses a very clear ideological position with regard to Trump, how this might be read will inevitably depend on what both Hall and Morley have characterized as the dominant, negotiated and oppositional stance of the viewer. A person critical of Trump would read this very differently from one who was supportive of his disruptive presidency, who might simply reject the image altogether as a piece of left-wing propaganda. This suggests that the history of media audience research still has much to offer the present as we wrestle with contemporary concerns about media content – many of which are merely the latest iteration of ongoing moral preoccupations.

A question of morality

For the moral campaigners of the 1920s who initiated the series of research projects known as the Payne Fund Studies, the representation of sexuality was a major concern, not to mention the potential dangers of congregation in the dark. Given the popularity of the movie theatres amongst young people, it was imagined that these images would also be having a profound effect on young people. As noted in Chapter 2, this inspired all kinds of inventive research methods to try and capture these potential effects, from psychogalvanic skin measures, to the collection of hundreds of individual biographies (Jowett et al., 1996, p. 81). While the Payne Fund Studies were by and large concerned with sexual matters, the other moral concern that would preoccupy media audience research from the 1960s onwards was the depiction of violence. Although this anxiety began with a concern about screen violence in film, it subsequently extended to television and video and thence to the home computer and the playing of video games. Echoing the use of psychogalvanic skin measures employed in the Payne Fund Studies, elaborate experiments were conducted by social psychologists in laboratory-type situations, often involving their own students, to test the kinds of effects that these games might produce. However, in a review of the audience research on 'violent video games' (conducted in 2010 for the Attorney General's Department in Australia), the authors argue that many of these studies were problematic because they included 'contested definitions and measures' both of what is understood by the term 'aggression' as well as the category 'violent video game'. For example, are sports games more or less violent and aggressive than games which feature fictional or real wars?

Another problem with this laboratory-type research was the fact that it often failed to consider in any depth other variables, including race, ethnicity, gender and other contextual factors. Indeed, as has been observed by many, there was a consistent bias in that the participants were often university students, who may not be typical of the game-playing population as a whole. Another issue had to do with the ways in which increased aggression may be measured using what are described as 'proxies' for aggressive behaviours – such as 'noise blasts', which are hardly indicative of how people might respond to frustrating incidents in real-life situations. The authors of this comprehensive survey therefore end with the kind of non-conclusive paragraph that is typical of attempts to review the literature on media effects:

Significant harmful effects from Violent Video Games (VVG) have not been persuasively proven or disproven. There is some consensus that VVGs may be harmful to certain populations, such as people with aggressive and psychotic personality traits. Overall most studies have consistently shown a small statistical effect of VVG exposure on aggressive behaviour, but there are problems with these findings that reduce their policy relevance. Overall, as illustrated in this review, research into the effects of VVGs on aggression is contested and inconclusive.

(Attorney General's Department, 2010, p. 42)

In other words, the jury is still out, although those who are described as 'causationists' remain convinced that experimental and quantitative measures have proven the case. Meanwhile, the incidence of school shootings and other mass murders in the USA continues, with the various administrations apparently unable achieve any form of gun control in the face of powerful lobby groups determined to uphold the Second Amendment of the United States Constitution: the right of every American citizen to bear arms. Rarely is the critical factor that there are more guns than people in the USA mentioned in the debate about the potential effects of exposure to media violence.

Interestingly, the use of scientific methods would appear to have made something of a comeback in industry audience research, as reported by Lene Heiselberg from the Audience Research Department of the Danish Broadcasting Corporation. In an article published in the journal *Participations*, Heiselberg describes how she and her team embraced a 'mixed methods' approach to test new programming with viewers. This included both a self-report questionnaire and skin conductance measurements in order to evaluate the conscious and unconscious reactions to 'emotionally engaging TV programs' that are often difficult for an audience to articulate (Heiselberg, 2018, p. 25). Rather than seeking to limit the emotional *affect* of their content, the goal of Heiselberg and her team is to help their producers make more *effective* and engaging programmes in a screen landscape where attention to the screen is a major commodity.

So while, on the one hand, we have contemporary media producers keen to *affect* their audience and to hold their attention, on the other we have the long history of media audience research that is concerned with what *effect* that *affect* might have in terms of thinking and behaviour. Once again, this is by no means predictable since everyone brings to the encounter their own personal history, experience and prior knowledge – and this is as true of someone watching a gangster film in the 1920s as it is of someone watching a Danish TV crime drama or playing a video game in 2018.

The return of the repressed

While concerns about the effect of exposure to violence in the media persist, they have taken something of a back seat in the contemporary media environment. Since the turn of the millennium, the content that has continued to provoke the most moral concern has been that which depicts sex and sexuality, especially as this relates to children and their access to new media platforms and technologies that allows them to access, make and share images that are considered pornographic or obscene, terms that have always been problematic. As McKee et al. (2008, p. 5) point out, the term 'pornography' was first used by art historians in the 19th century 'to describe the erotic paintings and statues found by the archaelogists who unearthed Pompeii and Herculaneum from the volcanic ashes that buried them in AD79': a comment that points to the often fraught and blurred distinction between the erotic and the pornographic that has haunted the representation of sexuality in art, in photography on film and online ever since. As feminist scholar Linda Williams points out in her groundbreaking history of pornography, *Hard Core: The Frenzy of the Visible* (1999), how pornography is defined and who gets to see it has long been the privilege of those with the power and moral authority to censor and control its circulation.

At time of writing in 2019, a year-long exhibition of photographic work by the controversial American artist Robert Mapplethorpe is opening at the Guggenheim Museum in New York. Entitled *Implicit Tensions*, the first part of this exhibition will feature 'classicizing photographs of male and female nudes; floral still lifes; portraits of artist, celebrities, and acquaintances; explicit depictions of New York's underground S&M scene, and seeringly honest self-portraits'.[6] It might be noted that when a retrospective of Mapplethorpe's work containing similar images began touring in the United States shortly after his death in March 1989, controversy dogged the show, culminating in the police pressing charges of obscenity against the Contemporary Arts Center of Cincinnati (Sullivan and McKee, 2015, p. 136). The images in

---

[6] https://www.guggenheim.org/exhibition/mapplethorpe

question included one of Mapplethorpe himself with a bull whip inserted into his anus and portraits of two children with their genitals on show. In this case, the defendants were acquitted, with the jury finding that although the images in question were in fact 'obscene' they also had some 'artistic merit', a decision that highlights the arbitrary nature of the line that divides pornography from other forms of artistic expression.

More recently in Australia, in 2008 photographs by the acclaimed artist Bill Henson were also 'seized' by police from Roslyn Oxley9 Gallery on the grounds that these constituted child pornography (Sullivan and McKee, 2015, p. 137). The then Prime Minister of Australia, Kevin Rudd, subsequently appeared on television denouncing these images of prepubescent young people as 'offensive and disgusting'. However, a 'storm of protest from the art world' eventually led to the charges being dropped and the artworks were returned to the gallery. As Sullivan and McKee note, while many scholars have used cases like these to explore 'the nebulous distinction between art and pornography', in effect this leaves the legal concept of obscenity dependent on a value judgment that is usually made by an economically and culturally privileged community of art scholars and judges (Sullivan and McKee, 2015, p. 137). In each of these cases it is the 'interpretation' of these images by the privileged few that will determine their status.

While these test cases tend to hijack the debate about representation of sexuality when it comes to 'ordinary' people and their consumption of pornography, there have been very few studies that have attempted to discover the value of such content for them. As Alan McKee, Katherine Albury and Catharine Lumby (2008, p. 25) discovered in their ground-breaking study of mainstream and legal pornography in Australia in 2003, far from being a minority pursuit, according to a Roy Morgan survey at that time about 33 per cent of adult Australians were likely to access some form of sexually explicit material in the course of their lives. Nor did these people fit the unfortunate stereotype of the deviant, sad or lonely porn consumer. As McKee et al.'s survey of 1000 porn users revealed, these people came from all walks of life, were married or in relationships as well as single, and could be of any age, although the largest proportion of their sample were in the age bracket 26 to 35 (McKee et al., 2008, p. 27). Furthermore, while the majority of respondents were men, 17 per cent were women, a number that is likely to have risen significantly since 2003 with the availability of porn online that allows women to access this in the privacy of their homes as opposed to the embarrassment of being seen accessing this in public (McKee et al., 2008, p. 27).

When asked about the effects of pornography on themselves as users, the top three reported outcomes were that watching pornography made people feel more relaxed and comfortable about sex, more open-minded and willing to experiment and more tolerant of other people's pleasures: a set of outcomes that might be described as positive and even pro-social (McKee et al., 2008, p. 85). While it is entirely predictable that people would choose to present their consumption of pornography in the best possible light given that they are aware of how they might be judged, these findings contradict many of the assumptions about the effects of pornography. As it is, this study reveals that audience research has much to offer when it comes to understanding exactly how people find value in the media content they consume and how they might account for this.

According to Brian McNair, over the course of the 20th century the media have played a significant role in a process that he describes as 'the democratization of desire' (2002, p. 11). This is a direct result of an erosion of the power of the state to censor and control representations of sexuality at the same time as new media technologies have given people access to the means to explore and express 'a more diverse and pluralistic sexual culture than has previously been accommodated within patriarchal capitalism' (McNair, 2002, p. 12). Written *before* the introduction of YouTube and the iPhone, McNair's exploration of how new media technologies have enabled ordinary people to produce their own sexual content is essentially optimistic about the democratic possibilities of these affordances. However, these same affordances precipitated a new wave of concern about the kinds of content that could be produced and shared by young people.

Sexting

Once again these concerns can be read as symptomatic of current social and cultural anxieties, particularly as these pertain to young people. As Ringrose et al. (2012, p. 9) suggest, the young are often positioned in the vanguard of new media developments, their experiences simultaneously encapsulating society's hopes for a better future as well as 'the risks and harms associated with technological change'. Defined by Livingstone et al. (2012) as 'the exchange of sexual messages or images' via text messaging, smartphones or social networking sites, sexting became the focus of much public attention during the early years of the 20th century, especially as this related to debates about the sexualization of children by the media industries. In Australia, this anxiety was fuelled by the release of a controversial and alarmist report entitled *Corporate Paedophilia* (Rush and La Nauze, 2006), which revisited concerns about advertising images and the content of girls' magazines to make a case that young people were being adversely affected by exposure to certain kinds of media representations.

While sexting is not an activity confined to young people, it is young people who have attracted the most concern about such activities in the UK, USA and Australia, where the legal implications of 'sexting' for minors might well include them being charged with possession of child pornography. As Albury et al. (2013) reported, there were over four hundred articles about sexting published in Australian newspapers prior to 2013, most of which focused on sexting as a crime or as an aspect of cyberbullying, with the frequent implication that young people are unable to navigate either their own sexuality or the new media technologies (Albury et al., 2013, p. 4). Thus, once again, it is possible to trace the connection between public concern as reported in frequently sensationalized newspaper reports and the commissioning of a number of well-intended research studies intended to investigate the issue.

These include the first qualitative study of sexting in the UK by a team of researchers led by Jessica Ringrose at the Institute of Education in London and sponsored by the National Society for Prevention of Cruelty to Children (Ringrose et al., 2012). This project began with the open-minded goal of discovering whether sexting was indeed a new kind of social activity or one that might be continuous with earlier forms of youthful sexual practice. The investigators were also concerned to establish just how widespread the practice might be and whether it constituted a potential harm or a benefit to those who participated (Ringrose et al., 2012, p. 9). The approach was therefore nonjudgmental in an endeavour to establish exactly what 'sexting' might mean to the young people themselves. As the authors were keen to point out, while there appeared to be an assumed 'weight of evidence' that young people were being 'directly sexualised' through their exposure to certain kinds of media content, in fact there was a severe shortage of 'rigorous research' on this issue (Ringrose et al., 2012, p. 17).

The research methods used included focus group interviews with 35 young people in years 8 and 10 in two inner-city London schools. The researchers also asked participants to 'friend' them on Facebook so that their online social activities could be monitored and mapped, although they soon discovered that Facebook was not the most important platform in these young people's lives. Indeed, their participants had already migrated to Blackberry Messenger (BBM) as their preferred platform because of its cheapness. The researchers thus had to learn all about the affordances of BBM that enabled both social networking and texting through the establishment of group networks on a mobile phone. A further 22 individual interviews were then conducted with the students as well as key teachers and staff at the same school in order to provide what is described as additional content and depth to the analysis.

What the researchers discovered were the intense affective bonds that the young people in this study had with their mobile technologies and the ways in which these were 'intimately entangled in the making and unmaking of young people's everyday lives and relationships' (Ringrose et al., 2012, p. 26). As one group of 14–15-year-old girls reported, their mobile phones were a constant companion from waking up in the morning to going to sleep at night. Another significant finding was the fact that sexting included a much greater range of practices and was far more prevalent in this cohort than previous assessments or research had suggested. In seeking to address the reasons for this, the researchers were therefore at pains to point out that it was vital to understand sexting within the context of these young people's everyday lives in school, and the impact of culture, class, race, sexuality and indeed gender on their engagement with the media (Ringrose et al., 2012, p. 25). The researchers were, in fact, stunned by the normalized sexism and sexual violence they encountered in the school that was played out in these online relationships. In other words, the mobile technologies available to these young people were being used to reinforce patterns of sexualized behaviour that also existed offline. As the authors concluded, both parents and teachers seemed to be remarkably and worryingly out of touch with the realities of these young people's social experience.

This 'out of touchness' was also the case in Australia where Albury et al. (2013) discovered that the young people aged 16–17 whom they interviewed did not even accept the term 'sexting', suggesting that this was an adult-generated word representing adult anxieties. The 16 young people in this small study were both puzzled and offended by the tendency for adults in general (and educators in particular) to place all naked or partially naked user-generated images into the category of sexting, preferring themselves to use the more neutral terminology 'pictures' (Albury et al., 2013, p. 8). A number of the young women in this study also suggested that adults appeared overly focused on the appearance of young women and resented the fact that they were being constantly monitored for signs of sexualization or provocativeness (Albury et al., 2013, p. 10). For both the male and female participants in this study, it was not nudity that made a picture offensive but the absence of consent in its production and distribution to a wider audience (Albury et al., 2013, p. 11). Indeed, the young people in this study were much more concerned with issues of privacy and the freedom to explore their sexual identity on their own terms. What was of most surprise to these participants, however, was the fact that although the legal age for sexual consent in Australia is 16, it is illegal to visually record any form of sexual activity involving young people of 16 or 17, with the result that those in possession of such images may well be charged with possession and/or distribution of child pornography. As the authors note, young people need to be informed about both their rights and their responsibilities under the law, while noting that the challenge for society may well be to resist the association of images of nudity, particularly female nudity, with inevitable 'shaming' or 'loss of reputation' (Albury et al., 2013, p. 17). The sharing of sexually explicit content, however, is hardly the whole story when it comes to how people are using the affordances of the new media technologies and platforms that have emerged since the turn of the millennium, as the case of YouTube reveals.

The YouTube experiment

Introduced as a video-sharing platform in 2005, during the first two years of its existence, YouTube was consistently framed by the mainstream press either as 'a chaotic and unregulated repository for a flood of amateur content' or as a big new player in the digital economy (Burgess and Green, 2018, p. 24). Two years later and YouTube had already disrupted existing media business models to eventually become a mainstream media industry player, with channels devoted to professionally produced content in addition to the amateur and 'vernacular' content which has always been its 'core business'.

In terms of the types of content being produced, in their 2007 sample of 4320 videos, Burgess and Green discovered that just over half of these were 'user-created', with the majority of these comprising 'vlogs' or video blogs (40 per cent). Given the direct address-to-camera nature of the 'vlog', Burgess and Green suggest that its early dominance as a category 'emphasises the persistent cultural importance of interpersonal face to face communication', inviting critique, debate and discussion (Burgess and Green, 2018, p. 81). Next in popularity were 'user created music videos' (15 per cent), 'live material' (13 per cent), informational content (10 per cent) and scripted content (8 per cent) (Burgess and Green, 2018, p. 66).

Eleven years later, according to Omnicore, a US-based digital marketing agency, by June 2018 more than 5 billion videos had been shared on YouTube, with 30 million people accessing the platform on a daily basis.[7] In terms of 'users', Omnicore reported that these are largely male (62 per cent), with 80 per cent of users coming from outside the USA. As for the types of content they are consuming, Omnicore suggests that 75 per cent of adults turn to YouTube for nostalgic reasons rather than tutorials or current events. More specifically, they suggest that males are primarily watching football or strategy games while females are watching beauty videos. This proposition would appear to suggest that while the ways in which people access content may be changing, what they are using it for may be stuck in a very traditional set of ideologies and forms of practice if these statistics are to be believed.

When it comes to the kinds of content that attracts large numbers of views, in 2018 YouTube's 10 Top Trending Videos attracting more than 673 million views were as follows (according to my trawl through the website in August 2019; YouTube, 2018).

1. **To Our Daughter** (80,607,091 views)[8] – a quasi-amateur documentary following the pregnancy and birth of American celebrity Kylie Jenner's daughter (11.32 minutes, published 4 February 2018).

2. **Real Life Trick Shots 2 'Dude Perfect'** (153,836,011 views) – a video of men throwing things by a group with their own YouTube Channel (4.17 minutes, published 22 January 2018).

3. **We Broke Up** (50,211,628 views) – an amateur vlog featuring heterosexual couple Lisa and David, with their own YouTube channel

---

[7] https://www.omnicoreagency.com/youtube-statistics/

[8] These viewing numbers were correct as of 14 February 2019. The original figures were not provided. Since the original publication of this list, number two has overtaken number one.

of comic encounters. Lisa now has her own YouTube channel where she also stars in an original comedy series (6.18 minutes, published 4 June 2018).

4. **Walmart yodeling kid** (63,197,529 views) – an amateur single-shot video of a 11-year-old Mason Ramsey singing unaccompanied. The YouTube sidebar then directs the viewer to his appearance on the Ellen DeGeneres Show, where he was granted his wish to sing at the country music concert Grand Ole Opry and presented with a $15,000 cheque towards his college education (2.02 minutes, published 1 April 2018).

5. **Do You Hear 'Yanny' or 'Laurel' (Solved with Science)** (52,054,381 views) – a science podcast explaining how sound travels at different frequencies (2.58 minutes).

6. **Portugal v Spain 2018 FIFA World Cup Russia** (68,409,325) – edited professional footage of the goals scored in this match (2.10 minutes).

7. **Build Swimming Pool Around Underground House** (91,807,987 views) – this video appears on the channel, Primitive Survival Tool, that has almost 3.6 million subscribers. It belongs to the genre of YouTube videos known as primitive technology, which demonstrate how to build things without any influence from the modern world.[9]

8. **KobraKaiep1 Ace Degenerator** (54,927,220 views) – a professionally produced YouTube premium drama based on the character of the losing fighter in the original *Karate Kid* film. The first episode is free (27.31 minutes, published 2 May 2018).

9. **Behan Bhai Ki School Life – Amit Bhadana** (42,912,809 views) (10.52 minutes, published 8 January 2018).

10. **NGƯỜI TRONG GIANG HỒ PHẦN 6 | LÂM CHẤN KHANG | FULL 4K | TRUYỀN NHÂN QUAN NHỊ CA | PHIM CA NHẠC 2018m** – the sixth episode in a popular gangster drama series produced by Lam Chan Khang, who is a singer and filmmaker. At time of writing he was only the second artist in Vietnam to attract 1 million subscribers. According to YouTube, this video was one of

---

[9] https://www.bbc.com/news/blogs-trending-45118653

the most watched videos in Vietnam in 2017 and is the first video from the country to make the global trending list.[10]

This list reveals the sheer diversity of the content available on YouTube, which ranges from the familiar and professionally produced (sport, drama and documentary) to new types of pro-am content such Real Life Hot Shots and Build Swimming Pool Around Underground House. The distinction between amateur and professional, however, is sometimes hard to make since amateur vloggers such as David and Lisa have now leveraged their careers on YouTube to enable them to become what Cunningham and Craig (2017) identify as 'professionalising amateurs'. As Burgess and Green suggest, these content creators routinely identify themselves as 'YouTubers', a label that signals both their membership of the YouTube community and the fact that for them YouTube also functions as a social media platform (Burgess and Green, 2018, p. 94). However, when it comes to understanding how people make and use content on YouTube, as on any other media platform, there is clearly the need for a more nuanced approach. As Burgess and Green suggest, 'Like all media, YouTube only really makes sense when understood in the context of everyday life' (Burgess and Green, 2018, p.72), as is evident in the ethnographic research of Patricia Lange (2014).

Over the course of two years from 2006 to 2008, Lange interviewed and followed 40 young people who were active on YouTube. This included 22 young people aged 9–17 and 18 young adults aged 18–26. Her methods also included participant observation, the analysis of video and text comments, online observations and YouTube 'meetups'. Her primary goal was to investigate the ways in which young people were using video to express the self, but she was also interested in the ways in which they might use their video skills to achieve a technical identity and to capitalize on their digital literacy. The types of user-produced content she encountered included live-action versions of computer games, casual footage of teens having fun on a hike as well as 'deeply felt video blogs about civic engagement' (Lange, 2014, p. 16). Lange is particularly interested in the type of content she describes as 'personally expressive video', content that enables the creator to communicate aspects of their self (Lange, 2014, p. 16). While such content may be only intended for close family and friends, or what Lange characterizes as the 'home mode', it is of course quite possible for this kind

---

[10] Facebook: https://www.facebook.com/khangprofilm?fref=search&__tn__=%2Cd%2CP-R&eid=ARA04uBg27iXrUdAdzKfOdnLXUUupu4q3DmLDClfk9_4mZ3jiPXcN2 48C_qRlO0oZQHxWSx5rONHrH0y

of content to 'go viral', as in the case of Mason Ramsey yodelling in Walmart. While the video of Ramsey singing was presumably shared with his consent, the creation of such amateur content may raise serious ethical issues about the exposure of unwilling and vulnerable participants, concerns that continue to fuel anxieties about YouTube as a lawless and potentially dangerous place for young people both in terms of what they create and share as well as what they might encounter there (Burgess and Green, 2018, p. 27).

In Lange's opinion, YouTube has become a kind of Rorschach mirror reflecting every viewer's own desires, fantasies and worst fears (Lange, 2014, p. 9). For example, when people described the kind of video they found most amusing or frightening, it was evident that these inevitably reflected their own particular interests and concerns: parents were worried about cyberbullying, college students were interested in celebrities and politicians talked about the power of social media to make a difference (Lange, 2014, p. 10). These observations thus support the contention that when making sense of the content that matters to media audiences, the social and cultural context of that audience once again has to be taken into account. Audience research, even when it is concerned with user-generated content on emerging media platforms, is always about people, as Chapter 5 will attest.

5 The People who Matter

Evidently there are some people who are of more interest and concern when it comes to the media they use and consume than others. However, while there are thousands of studies that consider those audiences who are perceived as 'vulnerable', such as children and young people, there are very few that address the media practices of those in positions of power, although the ways in which politicians use social media became increasingly significant following the 2008 election campaign of former US president Barack Obama and the late-night/early-morning Twitter activities of Donald Trump following his election in 2016.[1]

From an industry perspective, the differential attention accorded to disparate audiences might well relate to their potential value as consumers of both of content and advertising. In other words, the more spending power a specific audience may have, the more attractive they are as a potential audience to those seeking to profit from their engagement. As James G. Webster points out, the current media environment offers people countless choices in terms of the types of content they can access, with the result that producers of media are now competing with one another in what he aptly describes as 'the marketplace of attention' (Webster, 2014, p. 1). With the diversification of media platforms, people now have a much greater range of media content from which to choose, leading to the emergence of what one Foxtel executive described as a 'global micromarket' for certain kinds of Scandinavian-inspired crime drama (Turnbull and McCutcheon, 2019). Wealthy and well educated, this global micromarket is clearly a niche worth catering to, as evidenced by the creation of content intended to 'pull' them to a service for which they are willing to pay.

---

[1] https://www.nytimes.com/2008/11/10/business/media/10carr.html

When it comes to audience research that is concerned with a notion of the public good, most Anglo-American histories of the media begin with anxieties about the working-class audience in the 19th century. As Richard Busch notes, anxieties about the 'unruly' audience begin with that for popular entertainment, such as the music hall, and carry over to the behaviour of audiences at the cinema (Butsch, 2000, p. 4). Interestingly, this anxiety is not based on these audiences being passive, but rather on their potential for rowdiness and disruption. Central to these concerns are questions of taste, with a distinction gradually emerging between the preferences of the working-class audience and those of those middle and upper classes (for theatre, opera, 'serious' literature etc.). Indeed, the issue of taste is one of the undercurrents that has directed the flow of audience research throughout the 20th century (Bourdieu, 1984), alongside questions of morality and what is perceived to be in the public interest by those who have the authority to dictate what this should be.

There has also been something of a bias in audience research in terms of race and nationality, with white Western audiences in the Global North being the predominant focus. However, in the latter half of the 20th century attention has increasingly been directed to the ways in which audiences in different countries might experience the same media forms and content. In the 1980s, the global popularity of the popular American serial drama *Dallas* prompted two studies concerned with the show's reception in two different contexts: *Watching Dallas* (1982/85), Ien Ang's study of the audience in the Netherlands, and that of Liebes and Katz in Israel (1993). While Ang's study involved 42 people who responded by letter to her invitation, published in a women's magazine, as to why they liked this American serial drama about a wealthy Texan oil family, the primary focus was not on the cultural identity of the participants, but rather what kinds of pleasure the watchers derived from the series, taking into account its American origin.

Broadcast weekly in an evening prime-time slot, with high production values and attention to big business, as well as the more usual family melodrama, *Dallas* was very different from the more usual American daytime soap operas, attracting significant numbers of male viewers and a great deal of public commentary. As Ang points out, while the global popularity of *Dallas* was being negatively cast as an example of American cultural imperialism, she was keen to establish just how and why the show was being watched. What was it about the series that was so pleasurable for a global audience? What was it that audiences could relate to? In order to find answers to her questions, Ang placed a small advertisement in the Dutch women's magazine *Viva*, which read as follows:

> I like watching the TV serial *Dallas*, but often get odd reactions to it. Would anyone like to write and tell me why you like watching it too, or dislike it? I should like to assimilate these reactions in my university thesis.
>
> (Ang, 1985, p. 10)

There are a number of key points to be made about this invitation. The first is that it begins with the researcher identifying themselves as part of the audience in question, as someone who 'likes watching' *Dallas*. The second is that it is open-ended and unstructured in its approach to the gathering of data. Participants are simply invited to 'write a letter' in which they might express what they like or don't like about the show. Ang subsequently received 42 replies to her advertisement; all but three were written by individuals and only one was anonymous. There were, however, only three letters from men or boys, which is hardly surprising given the advertisement was placed in a woman's magazine.

While these letters provided the 'empirical basis' for Ang's analysis of the pleasures deriving from the show, she was keen to point out that they were hardly 'representative' of the way in which *Dallas* might be generally received, nor were they typical of a specific social category given that they came from people involved in a range of social occupations (Ang, 1985, p. 10). Ang therefore explains that she dealt with these letters simply as 'texts', analysing them 'symptomatically' to identify the 'discourses', the words and phrases, that people used to account for the pleasure they derived from a controversial piece of popular culture such as *Dallas* (Ang, 1985, p. 11). Ang does not elaborate on the precise nature of how this discourse analysis was undertaken, nor how she arrived at her main findings, but it is worth noting that such a discursive approach has become increasingly prevalent in media audience research and has become far more standardized and rigorous in its procedures. There are now many guides and tools, including the NVivo coding package, to help researchers undertake systematic coding and analysis of the qualitative data they collect.

Ang's key finding, supported by quotations from the letters, points to the inherent ambivalence of the viewing experience. This was evident in the ways in which viewers of the show were keen to express an awareness of, and even to distance themselves from, the manipulations of *Dallas* as a TV show at the same time as they also admitted to deriving various kinds of pleasure from watching it. As Ang notes, this would inevitably include the routine pleasure of being entertained by television in their own homes. However, while the letter writers did their best to describe the precise nature of the pleasures that they derive from the show it is apparent that they found this difficult to do. This leads Ang to the conclusion that the audience may not have access to the kinds of discourse they need to express in any convincing way what they like about a popular text that they know is looked down upon by others. In Ang's opinion, this includes an understanding of how the series enacts what she describes as 'a tragic structure of feeling'. That is, because the soap opera is structured as a never-ending melodramatic narrative, with all the reversals of fortune that this necessitates, the characters can never arrive at any point of closure or ultimate happiness: whatever a character tries to achieve, they will be inevitably frustrated. As a melodramatic narrative with its constant reversals of fortunes, *Dallas* as a text therefore expresses the inherent contradiction of human experience, the impossibility of reconciling our desires with our reality (Ang, 1985, p. 74).

One of the most important issues raised by Ang's study involves the ways in which the participants framed their viewing in terms of their knowledge about what kind of show *Dallas* was, and what watching it might mean in terms for how they themselves might be judged. For example, some of those who responded to Ang's request for comments expressed their 'dislike' for the show, even though they had obviously watched it. This was often expressed as a critique of its Americanness, its commercial appeal and its stereotypical characters, with the respondents enacting the kinds of 'anti-fan' processes identified by Jonathan Gray in 2003. In the process of expressing their resistance to these texts, according to Ang these letter writers were demonstrating an 'ideology of mass culture', using familiar arguments to dismiss the series as 'rubbish' (1985, p. 91). Other letter writers who liked watching the show managed their knowledge of such negative perceptions by adopting an ironic viewing position, enabling them to enjoy the show precisely because it was so bad. In this way, they too distanced themselves from the show in an endeavour to place themselves in a superior position (1985, p. 100). This left the lovers of the show in a tricky position, since they also had to negotiate the negative critique of the show in order to express how and why it appealed to them. In only a few cases did the letter writers adopt what Ang describes as a 'populist position', rejecting the 'morals of the ideology of mass culture' in order to defiantly justify their own preferences and tastes (1985, p. 115). This leads Ang to a brief discussion of aesthetics, in particular the notion of a 'popular' aesthetic, which according to her reading of Bourdieu (1984) is deeply anchored in common-sense values and the recognition of pleasure (Ang, 1985, p. 116).

I've dealt with this study in some detail because it illustrates so well the problem of media audience research when it comes to making sense of what people say about a media text. For example, while it is clear that Ang never met her correspondents in person, her letter of invitation references her 'university thesis', thus signalling that she is a student in an academic institution. This raises the question of how the letter writers might have perceived Ang as a correspondent and how the expectation that she might judge their responses from an 'academic' position might affect the nature of their responses. While the precise impact of such an expectation remains unfathomable, it is important for anyone conducting any kind of media audience research to be aware of how the study is framed and how their own role within it may condition the responses of those who are participating.

In the *Export of Meaning*, Liebes and Katz were also concerned with the global reception of *Dallas*, in particular among different ethnic groups in Israel – as well as with American and Japanese audiences – arguing that these different audiences interpreted the programme in very different ways according to their ethnic and cultural background (Madianou, 2014, p. 446). Madianou perceives this as a problem since the perceived differences in the reception of the show are always grounded in, or related back to, ethnicity and culture, while no attention is paid to gender, age or other social, economic and political factors. In other words, cultural identity is constructed as *the* defining element that shapes the audience's experience of the show rather than any other political, social or economic factors. In Madianou's opinion this is dangerous since it risks a form of essentialism by reducing audiences to their cultural identity (Madianou, 2014, p. 446). Indeed, essentialism is an accusation that could be launched at any research that imagines the audience only in terms of one dimension, whether this be age, class, gender or attachment to a specific media form or practice.

Another significant study that considered media reception in terms of ethnicity, but that demonstrates a rather different starting point, is that of Marie Gillespie (1995). While for Ang the starting point was the text (*Dallas*), for Gillespie her engagement began with the people involved, a particular diasporic group of young Punjabi people living in South London. As a schoolteacher who had taught in the area for some time, Gillespie was interested in her students' media consumption in general and, in particular, their television viewing and how this might relate to their social identity. In Chapter 2 of her book, Gillespie discusses in considerable depth the precise nature of her ethnographic approach, outlining the various phases of her research, which extended over four years. In the context of recent debates about the appropriation of ethnographic methods in the emerging field of cultural studies (Nightingale, 1989), Gillespie was keen to establish that her approach was indeed anthropologically sound, as she describes how she 'immersed' herself in the field, sharing the lives and experiences of her informants on a daily basis (Gillespie, 1995, p. 62).

While Gillespie was interested in the role of the media in the lives of the young people she was studying in general, she soon discovered that even though the main type of regular family viewing leisure activity involved the watching of Hindi movies on video, the most popular television programme amongst all her respondents, both male and female, was the Australian soap opera *Neighbours* (1985–). According to Gillespie, for the young Punjabi people of Southall, the regular watching of *Neighbours* gave them a sense that they were part of a wider youth culture, one that was both national and international rather than being defined by their specific ethnic and local identity (Gillespie, 1995, p. 96). This was underlined by the fact that as some of the participants revealed, their parents were suspicious that watching *Neighbours* was encouraging their sons and daughters to become less Indian and more 'white'. As Gillespie notes (1995, p. 98), many of the parents considered that their family and cultural values were being undermined by soaps like *Neighbours*. For these parents, the main function of these shows was to alert them to the temptations of Western culture to which they feared their children might succumb.

Building on her extended participant observation, conversations and interviews with the young people in this longitudinal study, Gillespie was able to construct a convincing argument about the significance of *Neighbours* for these young Asian Londoners. This was based not only on what they said about the show, but how they watched it and how it appeared to relate to their everyday lives and experience. According to Gillespie, much of their enjoyment derived from a perception that there were many similarities between life on the fictional Ramsay Street in *Neighbours* and their own lives in Southall. Most importantly this involved the importance of 'talk' and 'gossip' in the management of their community, a practice shared by both the male and female participants in the study. Conversations about the characters and events frequently resulted in what Hobson identifies as 'collaborative readings' of the text (Gillespie, 1995, p. 145). Inevitably, such collaborative readings helped to cement the various friendship groups, especially when this enabled the discussion of the kinds of topics that would be taboo in their parents' company (Gillespie, 1995, p. 147).

Interestingly, conversations about *Neighbours* also extended to a discussion of the 'double existence' of the characters as actors whose images were circulating across a range of diverse media texts, including the inevitable gossip magazines (Gillespie, 1995, p. 143). This enables Gillespie to locate the experience of watching *Neighbours* within a transmedia environment in which viewing the show is only one part of the mediated experience of the text. This is an important point, in that it once again underlines how the audience relationship to the text in question has to be considered in relation to the other texts and transmedia experiences they encounter.

Gossip, as represented in *Neighbours* by the character of the interfering Mrs Mangel, was generally condemned by the young people in the study for the ways in which it could be used as a form of social control. In their opinion this was as true of the gossip on *Neighbours* as it was in their own experience of community, especially when it came to the surveillance of gender relations (Gillespie, 1995, p. 150). For the young men, but especially the young women in this study, gossip was directly linked to the concept of *izzat* or family honour, which they perceived to be an overriding and restrictive preoccupation of their parents. These young Punjabi people were therefore particularly interested in how the young people portrayed on *Neighbours* stood up for themselves in disputes with their elders and appeared to have significantly more freedom and control over their lives than they themselves. As Gillespie concludes (1995, p. 174), watching *Neighbours* and talking about it in their peer groups thus enabled these young people to compare their experience of family and community with the 'white culture on the box'. As she goes on to speculate, watching *Neighbours* would 'undoubtedly' contribute to their 'consciousness of cultural difference' and encourage them in their 'aspirations towards change' (Gillespie, 1995, p. 174). This, however, remains a conjecture, since social change may be the result of many immeasurable factors.

Gillespie's research was published in 1995, at a time when the 'steady' relocation of 'ethnic' migrants into developed nations simultaneously drew attention to the growing diversity of national populations as well as revealing the ways in which the transnational flow of media content might enable new cultural insights (Athique, 2016, p. 8). As Adrian Athique points out, this was the impetus for a range of studies (including Gillespie's) that considered the media use of 'minority populations' and the ways in which their media consumption might impact their construction of social identity and their assimilation or alienation (Athique, 2016, p. 10). While this might well be true of the consumption of different forms of television content, including the ubiquitous reality TV, what is missing from this picture are the effects of networked computing and the rise of mobile and locative media that have enabled an array of 'audience configurations that are yet to be adequately formulated' (Athique, 2016, p. 8), although concerns about the impact of new forms of connectivity have certainly been apparent in more recent research on young people.

'Youth'

Children and young people, sometimes referred to as 'youth' (which during the 1960s and 1970s carried a particular set of negative connotations) have always been front and centre in debates about the potential impact of each new media form. In trying to explain the sustained focus on children, danah boyd (2014, p. 16), who chooses to write her name in 'lower case', argues that adult nostalgia may well be part of the problem. That is, adults tend to idealize the experience of childhood, forgetting the trials and tribulations that they themselves suffered. In seeking to regulate children's exposure to the media, adults are thus struggling to preserve a false notion of childhood innocence. However, as Nancy Baym suggests, displacing adult anxieties about children's safety onto the Internet and mobile phones may make those fears more manageable but does little to protect children, and it may keep them from realizing the benefits new technologies can offer them (Baym, 2015, p. 51). As is evident, in these debates the Internet is often cast as a dangerous space where young people may encounter all kinds of harm, not just in terms of the types of content they might consume but also the kinds of encounters with others they might have in this space. This anxiety echoes the concern about young people and their experience of the movie theatres in East Harlem in the 1930s, as studied by Paul Cressey.

As for the types of content children might consume, histories of media and audience research often suggest that the moral preoccupation with mediated content began in the time of the Greek philosopher

Plato, who was worried about the type of stories to which the next generation of potential leaders might be exposed (Gray, 2003, p. 78). In his famous treatise on education, *The Republic*, written about 380 BC, Plato stages a discussion about the 'immoral poetry' of Homer and the need for censorship in order to produce the right kind of right-thinking person:

> [S]ome tales [about the gods] are to be told, and others not to be told to our disciples from their youth upward, if we mean them to honour the gods and their parents and to value friendship with one another.[2]

In a contemporary era when young (and much older) people are watching the screen exploits of superhuman gods in blockbuster movies inspired not only by Greek and Nordic mythology, but also a swag of Marvel and DC comics, one can only applaud Plato for recognizing just how enthralling such stories might be, even if he failed to realize that censoring them would only increase their appeal. What appears to have worried Plato most was the possibility that in the depiction of both the good and the bad young people might be attracted to the bad and seek to emulate such behaviour. This notion of *mimesis* (imitation) has underpinned anxiety about the potential effects of the media ever since. This anxiety, however, fails to account for the fact that moral choices are always made in a specific cultural and social context and are informed by individual cognition and psychology. Inevitably, this relates to how one constructs a notion of the individual who is also a member of an audience.

While concern about the potential harm of mediated content might begin with the epic poetry of Ancient Greece, as is evident from the preceding chapters, it has underpinned a vast array of media audience research, from the Payne Fund Studies in the early decades of the 20th century to concerns about the impact of the Internet, digital media and datafication in the 21st century. As has been observed, the young are often positioned in these debates as being in the vanguard of new media developments, their experiences simultaneously encapsulating society's hopes for a better future as well as 'the risks and harms associated with technological change' (Ringrose et al., 2012, p. 9). In this

---

[2] 'The Education of the Guardians', *Republic II and IV*, Sophia Project: Philosophy Archives, p. 11, http://www.sophia-project.org/uploads/1/3/9/5/13955288/plato_education.pdf

formulation, children routinely function as the proverbial 'canary down the mine', that hapless bird carried by miners to alert them to any dangerous gases that might be present in a tunnel by simply falling off its perch and dying. The most recent set of anxieties to feature children and young people as a media audience have been concerned with their engagement with digital media and the ways in which this may impact on face-to-face sociability, identity, creativity and other more sinister dangers.

For example, the Australian parenting website raisingchildren.net.au, on its page 'Healthy Screen Time and Quality Media Choices: 0–2', cites the recommendations of the American Academy of Paediatrics that children under 18 months should have no screen time other than video-chatting, while children from 18 months to 2 years can watch 'high quality programs or apps if adults watch or play with them to help them understand what they're seeing'.[3] Clearly this ban on screens rules out the possibility that children may actually be learning something at the same time as they build their digital dexterity. Meanwhile, as a casual media anthropologist, I have witnessed parents using mobile phones and tablets in public spaces such as restaurants to keep their toddlers occupied while they attend to other conversations or business, often also conducted on mobile phones. In other words, whatever the 'expert' advice might be, the ways in which children are being introduced to the digital media as a part of their everyday lived experience is changing, as is clearly evident in the following extended research project.

In 2006 Sonia Livingstone from the London School of Economics, along with researchers across Europe, launched the EU Kids Online Network. In its first phase, this project constructed a database of empirical studies relating to children's experience of internet and mobile activities. By 2014, this had grown to over 1500 studies (Ólafsson et al., 2014, p. 4). As noted in a summary of this research, two thirds of the studies involved quantitative data, with 60 per cent of those using samples that were intended to be representative at the national level (Ólafsson et al., 2014, p. 5). What was also apparent when reviewing this database was that there were very few studies looking at very young children and that too little was known in general about what children actually do online. Not surprisingly given the history of research on children as audiences, there was proportionally more research on the

---

[3] https://raisingchildren.net.au/newborns/play-learning/media-technology/healthy-screen-time-0-2-years

risks and harms associated with being online than there were on the opportunities and benefits (Ólafsson et al., 2014, p. 31).

In designing a framework for their own research, Ólaffson et al. (2014, p. 1) describe how they developed a multidisciplinary research framework as well as a methodological approach involving both qualitative and quantitative methods into children's online risks and opportunities. From 2006 to 2014 this project grew to include some 150 researchers in 33 countries across Europe, at the same time as access to the online world changed from being dependent on fixed internet access to one that includes the use of mobile devices and the ubiquitous use of social media platforms. In the online summary of the key findings of this research in 2014, the authors are keen to point out both the risks and the opportunities for young people online, noting that 'Not all risk results in harm.'[4] Indeed, only one in five of the 9–16-year-old respondents said they were bothered or upset by something they had encountered online. Although there was a slight increase in this concern since a previous study in 2010, the report suggests that the incidence of harm online is much less than 'many panicky media reports would suggest', leading the authors to the encouraging conclusion that the many safety and awareness-raising initiatives that have emerged around this issue in the countries involved must be proving effective.[5]

The executive summary to this report, however, points to the more positive effects of online engagement, since the first of the key findings suggests:

> The more children use the internet, the more digital skills they gain, and the higher they climb the: 'ladder of online opportunities' to gain the benefits.[6]

Nonetheless, the second key finding made the following more cautious proviso:

> Not all internet use results in benefits: the chance of a child gaining the benefits depends on their age, gender and socio-economic

---

[4] https://lsedesignunit.com/EUKidsOnline/html5/index.html?page=1&noflash#
[5] Net Children go Mobile Survey, https://lsedesignunit.com/EUKidsOnline/index.html?r=64
[6] https://lsedesignunit.com/EUKidsOnline/index.html?r=64#

status, on how their parents support them, and on the positive content available.[7]

In other words, it all depends on the social context of the child: a finding which echoes the conclusion of another famous audience research project concerned with the potential effect of a television on children, as noted in Chapter 2:

> For some children, under some conditions, some television is harmful. For other children under the same conditions, or for the same children under other conditions, it may be beneficial.
>
> (Schramm et al., 1961, p. 1)

In 2018 Livingstone, Mascheroni and Staksrud reflected on the three phases of the EU Kids Online research, arguing that their findings had served to debunk some of the prevailing myths and concerns about young people and the Internet. While this research had begun in an atmosphere of moral panic, a discourse of risk and censorious policy-making that led to the European Commission's first Internet Action Plan 1999–2002, by 2014 the debate had shifted away from *how* children engage with the Internet as a medium to how they engage with the world *mediated by* the Internet.[8] In this context, the online space is imagined as a space within which children learn to navigate in much the same way that they negotiate their everyday reality. The necessity of learning how to deal with threat, risk and unpleasantness is therefore as much a part of building resilience in the online world as it is in the physical world. In terms of a child's experience of audiencing online, what's interesting about the EU Kids Online project is that the only content to which it refers is the type of content that might cause harm, including violent/gory content, pornographic content, racist/harmful content and embedded marketing. What children actually enjoy, make and watch may be very different, as Patricia Lange discovered in her study of *Kids on YouTube* (2014).

While Livingstone and her colleagues were researching children across Europe, American scholar danah boyd published the findings of an eight-year study into the 'networked lives of teens' in the USA,

---

[7] Ibid.

[8] Livingstone provides a useful overview of the project on the Kinds Online website, http://www.lse.ac.uk/media-and-communications/research/research-projects/eu-kids-online/hear-from-the-researchers.

intended to reassure 'those who worry about them – parents, teachers, policy makers, journalists, sometimes other teens' (boyd, 2014, p. x). boyd's methods did not involve surveys but a different kind of qualitative approach involving 166 formal and semi-formal interviews with young people in their homes, at school and various public settings. According to boyd, she talked with teachers, librarians, youth ministers and others who work with young people, and she 'hung out' with teens wherever she could locate them. In effect, boyd was conducting what might be described as a 'loose' form of ethnography that subsequently enabled her to present herself as an expert in the field. Paradoxically, one of her key messages was the fact that young people themselves are rarely heard from in debates about their media use. Her book, she argued, is therefore intended to provide the young people she encountered with an opportunity to make themselves heard (boyd, 2014, p. xi). While this is admirable, inevitably the young people's voices are heard only through the medium of boyd's text.

According to boyd, the problem of addressing youth engagement with social media is compounded by the fact that while many people talk about what they perceive as potentially worrisome behaviours, few people are willing to take the time to pay attention to what young people themselves say about their lives, both online and off (boyd, 2014, p. x). Indeed, boyd describes how she was inspired to write about these issues by a young man who begged her to explain his online activities to his mother, who considered that 'everything online is bad'.

One of the more poignant findings of boyd's research is that the young people she interviewed lead much more restricted home lives than in earlier generations and that this is one of the reasons that the Internet has become the place where they choose to hang out, to network and to meet people. For the young people boyd talked to, the challenge of negotiating one's public and private identity is now carried out as much online as it is off. This observation serves to underline boyd's argument that what young people choose to do online cannot be separated from their 'broader desires and interests, attitudes and values' (2014, p. 202); nor, one might add, from the social context in which they are embedded, which may well include such power relations as parental controls or, indeed, their absence. In terms of content, boyd's argument is that teens' online connectivity enables them to share and spread content through the use of links, reblogging or favouriting. Content can be also be forwarded, reposted or shared. In effect, boyd argues, the ease with which people can share media content online is both 'powerful and problematic', given that it can be used for rallying support for a good cause or to spread 'rumours' (boyd, 2014, p. 12).

This attention to social context is also apparent in the work of anthropologist Mizuko Ito and a group of researchers in Japan (Ito et al., 2006) exploring young people's use of their mobile phones. Roughly translated, the word for a mobile phone in Japanese is *'ketai'*, meaning 'something you carry with you', suggesting that this personal device is a constant and mundane presence in everyday life (Ito et al., 2006, p. 1). More specifically, in a collection of essays entitled *Personal Portable Pedestrian: Mobile Phones in Japanese Life*, Kenichi Fujimoto discusses how *ketai* have become a technology that reflects the intersection of a number of Japanese youth subcultures. These include the use of the latest J-pop (Japanese pop music) for ring tones and Japanimation (Japanese anime and anime characters) as background motifs for screens. For young Japanese people at that time, the *ketai* was therefore much more than just a communication technology; it could function as a good luck charm, an alter ego, a pet or even a fetishistic object (Ito et al., 2006, p. 87). Once again, it is worth noting that this research is now somewhat dated as the ways in which mobile phones are used has continued to evolve in tandem with online connectivity and the proliferation of apps and streaming services.

Gender

Within the history of media audience research there have been times when men and women have been considered separately, such studies revealing much about prevailing attitudes to the construction of gender and sexuality in different temporal and cultural contexts. For example, while girls and women have been studied largely in terms of how the media may affect identity formation and behaviour, when it comes to boys and young men, often labelled 'youth', there has been an ongoing focus on the violence that is associated with the performance of aggression and hyper-masculinity. As Graham Murdock suggests, by the turn of the 20th century, working-class adolescent boys had become the particular focus of 'respectable fears' and the potential effects of the media on them have continued to be a source of public concern from the early days of the cinema to the present (Murdock, 1997, p. 72). Once again, we can see how anxieties about the effects of consuming content that is considered harmful is consistent with the emergence of new media forms from comics –including American psychiatrist Fredric Wertham's memorable diatribe against the comic book industry, *Seduction of the Innocent* in 1954 – to film and video, culminating in the controversy surrounding 'video nasties' in the 1980s (Barker, 1984), and to video games. While ingenious laboratory experiments were invented to test the effects of playing violent video games, in most cases these have been debunked for a variety of reasons, not least the fact that the participants are often the students of the academic undertaking the research and the 'proxies' used to measure aggression (noise blasts etc.) were hardly convincing.

When it comes to girls and women, however, the focus of the research and the questions that have been asked have largely been to do with the ways in which media texts might impact on their identity and life choices. Indeed, the second wave of feminism in the 1970s precipitated a range of illuminating studies that focused attention on the kinds of media girls and women liked: studies that often walked a conflicted line between condemning the media text for its ideological assumptions and discovering the kinds of comfort and value it might offer. This tension is clearly evident in an essay by Angela McRobbie on the popular British girls' magazine *Jackie*, first published in 1982 (McRobbie, 1982).

It might be noted that McRobbie's concern about the patriarchal values enshrined in *Jackie* was based on her own semiotic analysis of the text informed by current critical studies inspired by the work of French philosopher Louis Althusser. In his essay 'On Ideology' Althusser outlined his theory of how the state maintained control through the operation of both the Repressive State Apparatus (including the government, the army, the police and the courts) and the Ideological State Apparatus, which included both the family and the education system and, most interesting for our purposes here, communication identified as 'press, radio and television etc.' (Althusser, 1971, p. 143). According to this formulation, the ideology of the media is controlled by the vested interests of the powerful and the state (van Zoonen, 1994, p. 24).

In 1987 Elizabeth Frazer published another study of *Jackie*, one that involved talking to seven very diverse groups of young women in order to discover how they might respond to a 'typical' *Jackie* story, one that enshrined all the ideological assumptions of which McRobbie was so critical. Here Frazer argues against a simplistic model of media effects, suggesting that the major mistake committed by theorists of ideology is to assume that there is only one reading of the text, theirs. What she found in her research is that there were many ways of reading the particular story in question. The girls in her study were critical of the class and gender issues as well as the value of the story as a fantasy in purely aesthetic terms, noting 'I've read better ones' (Frazer, 1987, p. 416).

When asked to discuss this story, the girls did so in ways that were both self-conscious and self-reflexive, demonstrating a level of understanding not only of the story but also of the genre of publications to which *Jackie* belonged (Frazer, 1987, p. 419). This led Frazer to the conclusion that the concept of ideology is 'unsatisfactory' since it would appear that the young women with whom she spoke were far from unaware of the ways in which popular culture so routinely presented them with entertaining fictions and fantasies that did not reflect their own experiences.

A similar trajectory in thinking about TV soap operas and their female audience can be traced in a line that runs from Herta Herzog's remarkable research on radio soap operas in the 1940s, through Tania Modleski's ground-breaking study *Loving with a Vengeance* published in 1982, to Mary Ellen Brown's study *Soap Opera and Women's Talk*, published 12 years later in 1994. As a German academic closely associated with the Frankfurt School based at Columbia University in New York during the 1940s, Herta Herzog's research into the immense popularity of the radio soap opera amongst women in America was underpinned by the same concern about the 'dumbing down' of the audience as had been expressed by Adorno and Horkheimer in *The Dialectics of Enlightenment* (1944). As Tamar Liebes suggests, Herzog's 'canonical' essay 'On Borrowed Experience' (1941) was in the vanguard of what was to become a feminist critique of 'women's genres' that would include both the soap opera and the romance novel as instruments of women's enslavement under patriarchy (Liebes, 2003, p. 45).

Using both questionnaires and interviews, Herzog set out to discover why women chose to listen to these shows and what kinds of pleasure they derived from them. In the process, Herzog identified three main types of gratification. These included the ways in which listening to these shows offered the women a form of emotional release, the ways in which the shows allowed for what she described as a 'wishful remodelling of the listener's "drudgery"', and lastly how the shows provided an ideology and recipe for adjustment to their situation (Herzog, [1941] 2004, p. 142). In Herzog's opinion, these shows therefore *helped* their female listeners accept their role as housewives and mothers by continually validating these roles on air.

Although Herzog's work has often been associated with the functionalist approach later identified as uses and gratifications, as Liebes has convincingly argued, her judgments were in fact much more in keeping with those of her fellow members of the Frankfurt School in that she was convinced that it was the female listeners' subconscious psychological drives that underpinned their attachment to these shows (Liebes, 2003, p. 48). In Herzog's opinion, her findings were evidence that the women who listened were alienated, lonely and self-pitying and driven by emotional forces over which they had no control (Liebes, 2003, p. 42).

Modleski's later study of TV soap opera (which also dealt with romance fiction and gothic novels), also considered the potential value these shows might have for their dedicated female audience in terms of reinforcing, or undermining, patriarchal values, although it should be noted that Modleski did not undertake any empirical audience research in coming to these conclusions. However, in 1994 Mary Ellen Brown published her findings into the ways in which soap operas might inform women's lives, proposing that the pleasure women derived from their soap opera 'fanship' lay in the kinds of 'discursive networks' that they created in order to talk about a programme specifically designed for them (Brown, 1994, p. 1). In order to demonstrate this, Brown interviewed a number of soap opera fans, and it is their comments and conversations that are used to demonstrate key points in her argument about the potential for subversive and resistive readings of the text. According to Brown's findings, soap operas can thus contribute to the process of change by 'generating a rethinking of the role of women in society' (Brown, 1994, p. 172).

Brown's attention to 'resistive readings' points to a rethinking of media audiences that can be located in two books published in 1989: *Understanding the Popular* and *Reading the Popular* (Fiske, 1989a, 1989b). In these companion volumes, John Fiske proposed a re-evaluation of the relationship between the audience and the text. In *Understanding the Popular* Fiske outlined his theory of the ways in which popular culture can become a site of struggle and resistance. Informed by the work of the French scholar, Michel de Certeau in *The Practice of Everyday Life* (1984), Fiske expanded on de Certeau's military metaphors to explore how 'the weak' might use 'guerrilla tactics' against the strategies of the powerful, making 'poaching raids upon their texts' and playing constant 'tricks' against the system (Fiske, 1989a, p. 33). It might be noted that Henry Jenkins' later book, based on his own experience as a fan of *Star Trek*, *Textual Poachers* (1992), borrows its title from de Certeau's work. In seeking to illustrate what these guerrilla tactics might be, Fiske once again offers the example of the then popular American TV soap opera *Dallas*, suggesting that fans of the show might even read it *subversively* as a critique of capitalism (Fiske, 1989a, p. 44). Fiske's central point, however, is that any such subversive reading would always depend on how the 'socially situated reader' might interpret it.

Like Modleski, Fiske does not engage in any empirical audience research in any consistent way. Instead, his attention is firmly on the potential reading of a text which may be anything from a pair of jeans to the pop star Madonna. Fiske is thus primarily concerned with the ways in which these 'texts' can be analysed in order to expose their contradictions and/or their potential for political critique. Summarizing his argument about Madonna, Fiske therefore suggests that the pop star's appeal for her girl fans (whom he describes as 'wanna-bes') rests 'largely on her control over her own image' as well as her 'assertion of her right to an independent feminine sexuality' (Fiske, 1989b, p. 131). In Fiske's opinion, Madonna has thus adopted an 'oppositional political stance' that challenges patriarchal power in two ways – by insisting on control over her representation as well as her right to determine her own gendered identity (Fiske, 1989b, p. 131). Written in 1989, Fiske's comments about Madonna take on a new significance when compared to more recent debates about the female audience for the American singer and celebrity Beyoncé, who, like Madonna, has also inspired a number of academic books and articles (Trier-Bieniek, 2015).

In an introduction to a collection of essays that address the contested political impact and feminist potential of Beyoncé, Adrienne Trier-Bieniek (2015) suggests that ever since Beyoncé's appearance in the late 1990s as part of the all-female group, Destiny's Child, she has been a 'lightning rod' for scholars, feminist and critics alike. This would include American feminist theorist bell hooks (another academic who chooses to write her name in lower case), who, far from perceiving Beyoncé to be an empowering figure, described her as an 'anti-feminist' and characterized her self-presentation as a form of 'collusion in the construction of herself as a slave' (Trier-Bieniek, 2015, pp. 10–11). While these comments were controversial, and prompted considerable debate about exactly how Beyoncé might be perceived by her fans, Jessalynn Keller and Jessica Ringrose (2015) in the UK were engaging with what young women themselves thought in order to establish how they might be reading Beyoncé.

As part of a research project exploring the practices of eight US-based feminist girl bloggers and interviews with members of a high school feminist club in Wales, Keller and Ringrose discovered that the young women in their study had a highly nuanced understanding of celebrity feminism and a clear appreciation of the complexity of the issues involved. As one of their participants noted:

> She [Beyoncé] does empower women, but for example when she sung 'Who Run the World' which is all about women being strong

and women can do it and we're better than you guys ... she's in this really skimpy dress that shows her boobs and her legs.

(Keller and Ringrose, 2015, p. 133)

On the other hand, there were also comments about the ways in which Beyoncé marketed herself though her 'corsets' and her 'sexual dancing', with the comment that 'even if she wanted to be a feminist at heart she couldn't be because her being a brand doesn't allow her to' (Keller and Ringrose, 2015, pp. 133–134).

Keller and Ringrose conclude on a note of 'hopefulness', arguing that the young women in their study are 'shaping their own debates, producing their own media, and negotiating the contradictions presented by celebrity feminism with a great deal of wit and sensitivity' (Keller and Ringrose, 2015, p. 134). It would therefore appear that these young women are indeed exhibiting the 'active' characteristics of the audience as identified by Fiske. This is hardly unexpected, however, since this group of young women were already active in terms of feminist debate and blogging before the research took place. This study thus serves once again to illustrate how academics 'create the objects they set out to analyse' not only because of the ways in which they may frame the research question, but also because the selection of a specific audience to study will inevitably shape the findings (Ruddock, 2013, p. 8). This is particularly true when we come to that branch of media audience research that is concerned with fans.

Fans

Nowhere is the issue of audience identification and construction more significant than in the evolution of the field of fan studies, since such studies usually concern themselves with what might be described as a 'ready-made' audience with a shared interest or commitment to a specific media 'text'. As Jonathan Gray argued in 2003 in an essay that was critical of the state of fan studies at the time, fan research appeared to have overtaken audience research largely because of the fact that it is both institutionally and personally 'convenient', given that fans constitute an already self-identified audience for a specific media phenomenon, not forgetting the fact that so many academics appear to be fans of the phenomenon that they themselves are investigating.

As Daniel Cavicchi points out, treating fandom as a response to the mass media has tended to be a limiting move that excludes those who are 'fans' of the opera, museum-going or even novel reading (Cavicchi, 2014, p. 52). Indeed, fanlike attachments are evident in the followers of the Romantic poet Lord Byron, who wrote him admiring letters: letters that have been archived and preserved. Another telling example of 19th-century fandom would include the pilgrims who arrived in London in the 1890s looking for the home of Arthur Conan-Doyle's fictional detective Sherlock Holmes, only to discover that 221b Baker Street had yet to be built. As a fan of the Beatles in the north of England in 1963, I joined their fan club through a subscription via a post-office money order and was treated to monthly printed newsletters and an annual Christmas greeting recorded on a floppy vinyl disc before my passion wore thin and I transferred my attention to the Rolling Stones.

While fandom may predate fan studies, in their overview of the more recent field, Gray, Sandvoss and Harrington (2017, p. 2) identify 'three waves', with the first clearly inspired by the interventions of Fiske (1989a, 1989b) and Henry Jenkins (1992) in the 1990s. According to Gray et al. this era of research characterises fandom as a tactic of the disempowered, uniting people in communities of interest as a form of subversion as well as potential activism, and can be characterised as the 'Fandom is Beautiful' moment (2017, p. 3). The second wave, they suggest, derives inspiration from the work of the French sociologist Pierre Bourdieu and is primarily concerned with the sociology of consumption and questions of taste (Gray et al., 2017, p. 5). Fan studies in this era pay attention to the ways in which fan objects and practices are shaped by their social context, or what Bourdieu identified as the 'habitus' of the fan. While this research is also concerned with questions of power, inequality and discrimination, Gray et al. (2017, p. 5) suggest that it has 'little to say about the individual motivations, enjoyment and pleasures of fans'. As a consequence, this second wave of fan studies highlights the replication of pre-existing social and cultural hierarchies within fan cultures and subcultures (Gray et al., 2017, p. 5). The third wave of fan studies, on the other hand, has sought to 'move the goal posts' in a number of ways, broadening the scope of fan studies research to include a wide range of different audiences and practices, reflecting what the authors describe as 'fandom's growing currency' in the online world (Gray et al., 2017, p. 4).

Fandom, it is argued, has now become an integral part of contemporary life enacted through fan discussion groups, websites and social media networks, with the result that the imagined and voluntary communities that people join through their various fan attachments have become an increasingly important resource in the formation of identity. In an era when the traditional markers of identity such as employment status, class, marriage and national belonging, as well as age, religion, sexuality and gender, are becoming increasingly unstable, the 'imagined' communities offered by fan attachments may be as important to a person's expression of their self as any other (Gray et al., 2017, p. 11).

Fan studies, it is argued, now encompasses a range of different topics, including, but not limited to:

- The study of anti-fans.
- Fantagonisms and conflict between fan groups.
- Changing forms of (digital) textuality.
- The role of paratexts.
- Reception and value in fandom.
- The interplay between space, place, belonging and fandom.
- The role of fan identities, experiences and practices in the life course.
- The intersection of fandom and formal and informal political processes and activism.
- Forms of fan-generated content.
- Fan productivity.
- The eroding boundaries between media production and consumption.

Viewed from this perspective, fan studies include not only an engagement with popular culture but also politics, with fans having far greater potential for production and participation as well as consumption. For example, in the case of the Hulu television series *The Handmaid's Tale* (2017–) fan-like practices such as cosplay were rapidly co-opted in the service of political protest and activism all over the globe (Boyle, 2020).

Based on an award-winning novel by Canadian author Margaret Atwood, first published in 1985, *The Handmaid's Tale* first appeared to great acclaim on the streaming network Hulu on 26 April, 2017 with the first series going on to win eight Primetime Emmy Awards, including Outstanding Drama Series, and a Golden Globe for Best Television Series. A second season followed in 2018, with a third in 2019. While critical acclaim is one form of audience response that can be measured and calculated, what is perhaps most striking about initial audience response to *The Handmaid's Tale* are the ways in which the iconography of the series, and its potential political relevance to contemporary causes, were taken up by activists globally.

Set in a dystopian future, *The Handmaid's Tale* represents a society in which human reproduction has become a problem for those in power. As a consequence, the Commanders in charge of the Republic of Gilead have recruited fertile women, known as the Handmaids, to serve as surrogate breeders for them and their wives (Wollaston, 2017). These women are effectively sex slaves, held in captivity with no control over their reproductive rights. Dressed in red enveloping cloaks, with white bonnets that function like blinkers, the Handmaids are disciplined by the Aunts in brutal ways. In episode 1, the character of Offred (Elizabeth Moss) is kidnapped and removed from her family, and becomes the catalyst for a revolution in season 1 and a resistance movement in season 2. As is evident from the wave of protests that have borrowed from the iconography of the TV production, the issues raised by the series, including reproductive rights and the provision of health care for the poor, have resonated worldwide.

As Beaumont and Holpuch (2018) suggest, the premiere of the Hulu series coincided with efforts by US Republicans, 'emboldened by Trump's election', to roll back reproductive rights and health provision for the poor. As a sign of their resistance to these measures, in state capitals across the country silent women adopted the cloaks and the stark white bonnets of the Handmaids to protest against decisions being made by the majority-male representatives (Beaumont and Holpuch, 2018). Such protests have been echoed in different places and different contexts. Amy Boyle (2020) suggests that there have been *Handmaid*-inspired protests in 11 different countries thus far in relation to a number of different issues, including female reproductive rights, male violence against women, and the rise of misogyny and the conservative far right in government. This would include protests in the USA against Brett Kavanagh's supreme court confirmation hearing in 2018.

Whether the protesters who assume the garb of the Handmaids are fans of the show or not, this type of audience activity begs the question, what is the difference between fan studies and audience studies? To answer this question, I want to go back to Gray's essay on the anti-fan written in 2003, in which he argued that while much recent work on fandom continues to show the cultural relevance and complexity of fandom, 'the fan cannot and should not serve as textuality's default magic charm'. Researchers, he argues, need to go looking, 'microphone in hand', for different types of audiences and, with them, different types of textuality' (Gray, 2003, p. 79). But what exactly does Gray mean by 'different'? Who and where are the audiences that have been neglected and overlooked?

Missing in action?

Searching through the index to the *Handbook of Media Audiences* it is clear that there are a number of different ways in which an audience might be defined that are not included here. This would include audiences defined by their sexual orientation, such as Lesbian, Gay, Bisexual, Transgender, Queer or Questioning and Intersex (LGBTQI),[9] as well as audiences who are disabled in some way, indigenous audiences and older people. Audiences sharing these features, however, have always been present in the media landscape – as is being increasingly recognized and addressed in the new millennium. For example, as an urban geographer, Scott McKinnon (2016) provides a vivid account of the ways in which cinema-going played a vital role in the formation of a sense of community amongst gay men in Sydney from the 1950s onwards. Using a variety of eclectic sources, including film reviews and media reports, as well as personal memoirs and oral histories, McKinnon offers a detailed and telling account of how the practice of film-going and the experience of seeing a range of specific films helped to establish communities of interest and activism amongst the gay men in Sydney. Here a media form, a series of texts and a practice come together in a politics of identity that is linked to social action.

When it comes to disabled people, as Karen Ross noted in 1997, while at a conservative estimate one person in eight in the population of the UK has some form of impairment, and one in four families include a disabled child, research work with disabled audiences has rarely been undertaken (Ross, 1997, p. 669). This lacunae, she argues, has resulted in a series of unknowns, including how disabled people 'regard the portrayal of disability and disability issues' and how they feel about their marginalization or what they might want from broadcasting. After conducting 33 focus groups involving 384 people as well as 184 postal questionnaires, Ross set out to answer some of these questions, noting that while the sample might not be 'generalizable; the remarkable similarity in the views expressed suggested a number of significant themes. These included the observation that in general fictional media portrayals of disabled people often took a stereotypical line, making their disability their primary characteristic instead of providing a more realistic portrayal of the ways in which disabled people ran their homes, brought up families, and had loving relationships'

---

[9] As defined on the website of Akron University, Ohio, http://uakronstudentlife.orgsync.com/org/lgbtu/lgbtqi_definitions

(Ross, 1997, p. 671). When it came to non-fiction media, including news reports, the story was not much better, with a complaint that too often non-disabled experts were given the primary role in discussions about disability and disabled people frequently characterized as 'tragic but brave' or 'dependent and helpless' (Ross, 1997, p. 674). It might be noted that this research predates the advent of Web 2.0 and the opportunities this has afforded disabled people to form communities of interest and advocacy on the Internet and to produce their own content.

Indeed, the advent of Web 2.0 has enabled many hitherto marginalized audiences to find each other, speak up and insist on a recognition of their needs and interests. In this particular instance, we can see that audience research might well have a particular value for those who have hitherto been 'missing in action' from the field.

6 The Madness in our Method

When pondering the future of media audience research, why we should do it and how we might go about it in the 21st century, I flashed back to a panel on the topic at a cultural studies conference in the 1990s. As we prepared to make our presentations, the senior academic chairing the event announced somewhat testily, 'I wish audience research would just go away.' I bristled, but empathized with her irritation. Audience research is a messy and frequently frustrating business – rather like life itself – and it hasn't got any less messy as time has gone on, despite the frequent calls for more rigour and more consensus on priorities in the field (Barker, 2006; Morley, 2006; Press, 2006). If anything, with the advent of ubiquitous digital devices and the chimera of big data the field of audience research has become even more confused and confusing. As Jonathan Gray and his co-authors point out in their editorial announcing a new era for the *International Journal of Cultural Studies* in 2019, as a result of the proliferation of 'interactive mobile digital devices the media now permeate and structure both our physical and our symbolic environments' (Gray et al., 2019, p. 6). Indeed, they may well 'read our fingerprints and recognize our faces, occupy our fantasies and dreams, put us to sleep, wake us up, locate us, remind us, record us, promote us, entertain us, inform us, excite us, distract us, and even monitor us' (Gray et al., 2019, p. 6). The media, understood in a very broad sense, are now 'omnipresent' and we are 'bereft' when they are not. There's even a new word, 'nomophobia', to describe the 'irrational' fear of being without a mobile phone or being unable to use it in some way. While this might certainly be the case in those parts of the world where people have access to interactive mobile devices and reliable infrastructures, in the context of this book it seems relevant to ask at what point in all this ubiquitous media activity are we 'audiencing' as opposed to just using our digital devices to navigate through our daily lives? And is there a difference?

For example, sitting at my desk in the morning I may check my bank balance, write and reply to emails and organize my lecture slides that include a relevant and engaging YouTube clip from a web series comedy. Checking out the clip, I am encouraged by YouTube's suggestions in the sidebar to watch other related clips before I wend my way back to the next bureaucratic task in hand. As far as YouTube is concerned, I've just joined the YouTube audience: as I well know, I've been procrastinating by having a look around to see what is there or, as Annette Hill (2018) might say, I've been 'roaming' – a concept that echoes the notion of nomadic subjectivities and audiences debated by Radway (1988) and Grossberg (1988) in the 1980s.

Studying a media audience has always been a challenge given that it begins with the problem of defining and locating an audience that is constantly on the move and frequently out of sight. Gathering an audience for the purpose of research is therefore not unlike herding phantom cats, unless, that is, the cats/the audience have already congregated in a place where they want to be and you can actually locate them. This, of course, is one of the main reasons why fan studies has become such a vigorous branch of audience research, given that fans tend to congregate in virtual as well as real spaces to share their experiences. So while audiences may indeed assemble for a specific media event, text or personality, or around a particular website or hashtag, the practice of audiencing may also be nomadic, distracted and fragmented some, if not all, of the time. This suggests that what we are dealing with is a continuum of attention, with the casual and distracted nature of audiencing at one end and the more attentive and engaged audiencing at the other.

As compelling evidence of the fact that people *do* still assemble as an audience for the same content, if not always in quite the same time or space, the final season of *Game of Thrones* on the pay TV service Foxtel commenced in Australia on Monday, 15 April at 11 am. While this was admittedly an odd time for a 'prime-time series' to appear, this was necessitated by the significant time difference between Australia and the East Coast of the USA, where it would screen at 9 pm on the Sunday night. The imperative that Australians be able to watch the series at the same time as the American audience was created by the fact that, frustrated by the time delay in previous seasons, Australian audiences had found ways of downloading the series illegally. Indeed, during season 4 it was reported that while half a million viewers had paid to watch the show, another half a million had downloaded it illegally (Harvey, 2014). Marking the start of the last season in April 2019, the *Sydney*

Morning Herald ran no less than three stories on the series. One article in the business section suggested that this was 'arguably the last example of event TV on a mass scale', noting that few programmes 'beside live sport compel people tune in and watch TV at the same time in their own countries, let alone around the world (at often inconvenient hours)' (McDuling, 2019). Two articles were by television writer Michael Idato, who characterized the series as 'a sort of *Dungeons and Dragons* meets *Dallas*' (2019b) before proceeding to argue that 'what the Beatles are to music, *Game of Thrones* has been to television'. This seemed just a tad inappropriate, since it might be more reasonable to compare the success of *Game of Thrones* with that of other, more recent blockbuster fantasy franchises such as *Lord of The Rings* or *The Hobbit*: film trilogies that gave rise to a number of global audience studies (Barker and Mathijs, 2008; Michelle et al., 2017) as well as extensive debate about the best methodologies to use for this kind of large-scale research.

Although the *Game of Thrones* experience would appear to suggest that video on demand services are capable of assembling large audiences for a global media event, according to Chuck Tryon they also enable people to construct 'deeply personalized media environments' (2013, p. 5). Tryon portrays this personalized potential as a significant problem since these environments enable people to consume texts that they have self-curated based on their personal tastes, interests and politics. This self-curation is an affordance of successful platforms, such as Netflix, that are able to track their subscribers' habits via algorithms while 'pushing' more content that is specifically tailored to their preferences (Lobato, 2019, p. 41). The anxiety about media audiences that then arises is that people's choice of content will become more and more circumscribed. Thus, far from being exposed to the vast diversity of media and opinion in circulation at any one time that might challenge their thinking and assumptions, people are being exposed to, or opting for, more of the same. One of the presumed effects of this self-curation is that audiences will continue to consuming content that accords with whatever tastes or convictions they might already hold dear. As a result, they may be operating in what have been described as ideological echo chambers or filter bubbles, although a recent study by Dubois and Blank (2017) suggests this is unlikely.

It is important to note that anxiety about increasing insularity and individualisation (or atomisation as it was termed in the early days of television audience research) presupposes that people's encounters with media content is always personalized and that they are never exposed to any tastes but their own – a scenario that is predicated on a very limited view of the experience of media audiences. Indeed, one of the challenges for media audience research in the 21st century might well be to discover the range of audience experiences that any individual might encounter in any one day: a challenge that would indeed necessitate a non-media-centric approach to the study of media practices in the management of everyday life (Couldry, 2012). As Shaun Moores convincingly argues, such an approach is required because it is increasingly hard to separate out our media audiencing practices from all the other media activities we undertake in a day, especially 'since their embedding in the day-to-day contributes significantly to their meaningfulness' (Moores, 2018, p. 4).

For example, in addition to media roaming at my desk, in the evening I will settle down to watch my favourite Scandinavian crime drama on a free-to-air streaming platform of the Australian public service broadcaster, the Special Broadcasting Service (SBS). This is part of my daily ritual, an hour of drama before I go to bed. As I watch, while I may well be alone, I am aware that I am part of a global audience for this show even though I have no immediate experience of my fellow audience members. Audiencing, paradoxically, is therefore something we may do in private and we may not experience ourselves as part of an audience until we are 'hailed' in some way by the platform on which we are viewing, or we encounter others who have shared the same experience. Netflix, for example regularly 'hails' me as I check in, and I have now added our dog to the profile list of audience members in the house so that he too might receive recommendations based on his attention to the television series *Planet Earth* (2006) or the film *The Jungle Book* (2016). I could, however, easily locate some fellow viewers online, or through other forms of social encounter, should I wish to share my audiencing experience in some way. As a media audience researcher, I might then choose to assemble this 'found' audience of viewers for the purposes of my research. There is, however, clearly a difference between the audience that exists 'out there' and the audience that is assembled specifically for the purposes of research. At which point we might pause and ask, what is the purpose of audience research? Why are we doing it?

Why and what for?

As the previous chapters have established, media audiences have been constructed and researched over the years in a range of different ways for a variety of purposes. Audiences have been considered in relation to specific media technologies and platforms, in relation to specific content and texts and as a consequence of what are perceived as their defining characteristics, such as age, gender, ethnicity or taste. What this history also reveals is that this enquiry has been underpinned by a wide range of (sometimes conflicting) motives. This would include industry research that seeks to track audience behaviours for economic purposes, as well as research that is sponsored by private or government bodies motivated by moral or social concern for the audience's well-being. As Martin Barker has recently noted, 'audience research appears to get its kick start from moments when *cultural, moral* or *political* uncertainty sets in' (Barker, 2019, p. 2).

Revisiting a significant moment in the history of audience research in the 1940s, Elihu and Ruth Katz remind us of an important distinction that was made at that time between audience research sponsored by a particular agency, designed to help it do its work better and 'executed by means of scientifically acceptable methods', and research that was more interested in the larger context in which the audience experience is located. While the former was termed 'administrative research' and associated with the radio research of Paul Lazarsfeld in America, the latter was subsequently identified as 'critical research' and associated with the neo-Marxist critique of the 'culture industry' espoused by Theodor Adorno and fellow members of the Frankfurt School who relocated to the USA after abandoning their posts at the Goethe University of Frankfurt during Hitler's rise to power in Germany in the mid-1930s.

Katz and Katz therefore suggest that while administrative research is conducted in order to answer a specific question – for example a television station might want to know what kind of people watch reality shows and why – critical research would be much more concerned with why the TV station wanted to know, as well as the underlying motivations of the viewers. In the former, they argue, the viewer's responses may well be taken as 'face value', while the latter is more inclined to 'psychoanalyze' the responses and to explore the social implications of this kind of viewing (Katz and Katz, 2016, p. 8). According to Katz and Katz, the distinction between the administrative and the critical approach that divided these researchers in the 1940s is alive and kicking in media audience research 'today', even though it is quite possible to combine the two. In other words, researchers may combine an empirical approach to gathering data about what audiences say and do (at face value) with a critical approach (not necessarily psychoanalysis) that endeavours to place this in a larger societal context.

Academic audience research that illuminates how specific media practices are related to their social context has thus often served as a form of advocacy on behalf of the media audiences under investigation. This is particularly evident in the work of David Buckingham and Sonia Livingstone in the UK, or boyd in the USA, who have consistently advocated on behalf of the child and their right to be heard in debates about their media practices. It is also evident in the work of those who have conducted media audience research in relation to other marginalized and/or maligned audiences, such as research on viewers of pornography by Alan McKee et al. (2008). Another significant branch of media audience research has been motivated by a moral concern about the effects of the media, invariably constructed as negative, in relation to audience groups that have routinely been identified as being 'at risk'. In these instances, while such research is ostensibly motivated by a desire to protect the vulnerable, it inevitably advocates for some sort of regulation or control, including censorship.

Last but by no means least, audience research may also be undertaken out of curiosity and a desire to better understand human behaviour in relation to the media. Writing about transnational audiences, Adrian Athique (2016, pp. 12–13) reminds us of the work of the eminent sociologist C. Wright Mills and his concept of 'the sociological imagination'. According to Mills, this involves a set of cognitive processes whereby two opposing aspects of social reality – individual experience and the social structures in which this is embedded – are understood alongside each other (Mills, 1959, p. 8). This requires a 'vivid awareness of the relationship between personal experience and the wider society' as well as 'the capacity to shift from one perspective to another' and 'to range from the most impersonal and remote transformations to the intimate features of the human self' in order to understand the relationship between the two (Mills, 1959, p. 8). And it is this human capacity, Athique reminds us, that enables us 'to identify and understand the relationship between wider social forces and our personal actions' through the process of self-orientation (Athique, 2016, pp. 12–13).

The concept of self-orientation is important here, because it is assumed that this is something that people 'do naturally as social animals' (Athique, 2016, p. 13). This observation is significant because it draws attention to the importance of people's own insights into their media audience practices, how they make sense of what they do in relation to where they are in the world. While the Marxist response to this sense-making endeavour might well be that where people think they are may not be where they really are, evoking the spectre of 'false consciousness', how people might account for their media practices opens up the possibility of a conversation *with* audiences rather than a conversation *about* audiences. Such a conversation might then serve a very different set of purposes, leading to the question: can media audience research contribute to a process of self-orientation? Can it be of benefit to the audiences involved as well as to the researchers? Such a proposal inevitably has an impact both on the kinds of research questions posed, the methods that might be used and the kinds of impact audience research might have, in a current academic climate where accounting for the impact of academic audience research has become increasingly pressing.

Methodological moves

Over the last one hundred years, the methods that have been employed to undertake audience research have remained remarkably consistent, although the introduction of computers both enhanced and complicated the task of retrieving data and categorizing it. Indeed, looking back at the Payne Fund Studies as a point of origin, it is remarkable how ground-breaking they were in their eclectic mix of methods drawn from a range of disciplines, including the newly established disciplines of social psychology and social sciences. This included Ruckmick and Meyer's use of galvanic skin tests to measure arousal, Herbert Blumer's use of autobiographies and Cressey's sadly unpublished vivid ethnographic account of movie-going practices in East Harlem (Jowett et al., 1996).

Over the ensuing years, media audience research has routinely employed both quantitative and qualitative methods, often in combination, while social psychology has taken a different path, involving scientific laboratory-style experiments. Within 'mainstream' media audience research there now exists what I might describe as a 'classic' audience study. This will inevitably involve at least three different research methods to investigate the same phenomenon, following the now widely accepted notion that such triangulation 'vastly increases the researcher's confidence' in their findings (Priest, 1996, p. 254). Such a study might commence with a quantitative research method, such as a survey or questionnaire that includes both closed and open questions, that is used to identify larger patterns of audience behaviour. The data are then sorted and segmented in various ways, enabling the researcher to identify with some confidence the themes that will inform the next stage of the research. Stage two may then involve the use of more qualitative methods such as focus groups to identify the socially shared meanings that pertain, before embarking on a sequence of one-on-one semi-structured interviews to further explore individual perceptions of the specific themes, issues or attitudes that have been identified. The resulting account will then seek to relate the individual responses (illustrated by appropriate quotations) to the larger patterns revealed in the focus groups and the survey, in order to explain the ways in which this particular audience (that has been assembled for the purpose of this research exercise) might experience the media practice in question. Inevitably, all of these methods may be subject to considerable criticism, including the overarching problem that the way in which the initial research question was framed as well as the way in which the audience was recruited and the methods that were employed, will inevitably shape the findings. The findings, therefore, are not so much found as they are a consequence of the ways in which the study has been conceived and conducted. This, however, is the problem faced by all kinds of research, not just audience studies.

As David Sless pointed out, what is 'discovered' in such human-centred research all depends on the researcher's position in the 'landscape' of their enquiry (Sless, 1986, p. 33). In a landscape, Sless argues, 'the position one occupies determines what one can and cannot see, and what it looks like' (Sless, 1986, p. 33). That is, the perspective of the researcher, including all the research skills and intellectual baggage they may bring to the enquiry, will inevitably limit or enhance what they can see from the position they may adopt. And this is true even when their intention is to stand alongside those whom they are researching to try and see what their participants can see from their position in the landscape of enquiry. The researcher's perspective will therefore always be a function of the cognitive structures and concepts that underpin their research, as well as the methods used and how they interpret what they see, not forgetting the ways in which they choose to account for this. Undertaking audience research always involves interpretation, whether this be the interpretation of numerical data, what audiences say or even what they are seen to be doing. And yet calls for certainty and more theoretical progress in the field of audience research remain a constant refrain.

The 'Q methodology' debate

For Michelle et al., who conducted an impressive longitudinal study of the global audience for *The Hobbit* trilogy of films between 2012 and 2015, the way forward for media audience research involves a shared analytical framework, which they identify as the Composite Model (Michelle et al., 2017). This is the shorthand term for what is more properly labelled the Composite Multi-Dimensional Model of Modes of Audience Reception. Expanding on the analytical component of this 'Composite' approach, Michelle et al. propose that this involves four modes of audience engagement and response: the transparent, the referential, the mediated and the discursive. In the transparent mode, it is argued, viewers 'temporarily suspend disbelief and critical distance ... entering fully into the story to derive the specific forms of pleasure and enjoyment intended by the text's makers' (Michelle et al., 2017, p. 34). In the referential mode 'the text is primarily understood in relation to viewer's experiential knowledge(s) and perceptions of its relevance (or lack thereof) to the real world' (Michelle et al., 2017, pp. 34–35). In the more 'objective' mediated mode, viewers are described as focusing on the constructed nature of the media text as an aesthetic object, as a generic form or in terms of the industry-based imperatives that have contributed to its creation (Michelle et al., 2017, p. 36). The fourth mode is identified as a discursive mode in which viewers make sense of the text in relation to the messages it conveys about the world. Here Michelle et al. suggest that viewers may adopt one of the three reading positions as proposed by Stuart Hall in 1980 (p. 37), that is, the dominant/preferred, the negotiated and the oppositional reading of the ideological connotations of the text.

This extensive reception study, drawing on data garnered from 6500 respondents around the world, thus employs what the authors describe as a 'unique mixed-methods research design' incorporating a 'Q methodology' (Michelle et al., 2017, p. 28). The 'Q' methodology is described as a 'true methodological hybrid, combining the mathematical rigour of quantitative methods with a strong interpretive component more commonly found in qualitative approaches to human research' (Michelle et al., 2017, p. 41). Interestingly, it is noted that the Q methodology was invented by psychologist/physicist William Stephenson in the 1930s 'to analyse the nature and diversity of people's attitudes, beliefs, perspectives or subjective experiences relating to a given topic' (Michelle et al., 2017, p. 40). The adoption of this approach once again confirms the fact that media audience research has always been eclectic in its use of interdisciplinary methods.

What the Q methodology involves is inviting participants to rank-order a set of statements about the text that have been arrived at via 'extensive "cultural trawls"' of the 'wider discursive terrain or *concourse* around each film' (Michelle et al., 2017, p. 23). This concourse includes the major issues, themes and concerns that have arisen in public discussions of the films across print and online news coverage, media and film commentary, early professional and amateur film reviews, commentary on social media and key fan websites. This is arrived at through content analysis and what the researchers acknowledge as a degree of subjective bias in deciding which themes to select, although it is suggested that they sought to avoid this by using research assistants to do the coding, a curious claim since this assumes that the research assistants were also bias free. This concourse was subsequently whittled down to between 36 and 42 statements that the participants were invited to place into a ranked grid arrangement. This produced a number of 'factors' that were further explored using a conventional questionnaire with 'open-ended questions' that provided 'fascinating and highly revealing' individual responses (Michelle et al., 2017, p. 46).

While there is no doubt that this was a rigorous and robust research study, it essentially follows the 'classic' pattern already described. That is, it begins with a large-scale empirical data-gathering trawl, followed by a degree of categorization and sorting, before tunnelling down to the level of the individual in a quest to understand just how and why people responded to this trilogy of films in the way that they did. For Martin Barker in his thoughtful critique of the project, the degree of attention given to the respondents' comments is therefore of some concern given that in the final analysis 'quotations become illustrations, rather than opportunities for identifying discursive themes and repertoires' (Barker, 2018, p. 448). In Barker's opinion, the qualitative component of the research is thus reduced to that of a support role: that is, what people say is used to support the findings of the quantitative mapping of the concourse (Barker, 2018, p. 450).

Michelle et al. subsequently offered a spirited defence of Q methodology, pointing out that it has been adopted by an increasing number of researchers over time and that it offers a potential solution to 'the methodological and theoretical bottlenecks' (Michelle et al., 2019, p. 376) that have plagued audience research thus far: bottlenecks that inevitably include the relationship between the quantitative and qualitative dimensions of the research. In the case of Michelle et al.'s *Hobbit* project, this involved the segmentation of audiences according to their shared subjective viewpoints in relation to the concourse, rather than their socio-demographic characteristics (Michelle et al., 2019, p. 378). In the case of Barker and Mathijs' earlier *Lord of the Rings* project (in which I myself was involved as a researcher managing the Australian fieldwork), while this also involved the collection of 'prefigurative materials' including publicity and press coverage, these were dealt with independently of the globally circulated questionnaire that generated 24,739 responses (Barker, 2008, p. 222). In this study, it was the questionnaires that were the starting point for sorting the audience into segments and how they positioned themselves in relation to the film; different positions that were then explored by various researchers in different ways involving a diversity of approaches, an eclecticism that could be construed as (and was) either an advantage or disadvantage of the project as a whole.

Looking at these two significant large studies side by side, it is evident that both started with a research tool to assist in the identification and segmentation of their audience for the purpose of analysis. While *The Hobbit* study started with the 'concourse' of themes that people were required to sort in order to identify them as specific audience segments, *The Lord of the Rings* project used a questionnaire to categorize the audience in terms of their reception of the film. What was most important in the latter project, however, and I know this from my own involvement in the study, was that what people wrote in response to the open-ended questions enabled me to identify the ways in which some people within the Australian cohort of 551 expressed their 'disappointment' in the films (Turnbull, 2008a, p. 105), while others expressed their pleasure that was, paradoxically at times, 'beyond words' (Turnbull, 2008b, p. 181). In each case, it was the identification of the range of discursive responses in the questionnaires that generated the particular themes that were explored in more depth. This, of course, was not an unproblematic approach, involving as it did a close reading of what had been written in order to identify what appeared to be the key themes that might be significance and value. And, inevitably, every audience study ends up in an account that is framed by the perspective of the researcher.

So, while calls for more academic rigour, more reliable methods and consistent approaches may have haunted the field of audience research for decades, I'd like to suggest that the ways in which we evaluate the success of a research study that seeks to explore some aspect of media audiencing may have less to do with its methodology and more to do with how 'good' it is at explaining the phenomenon under investigation, while recognizing that there may well be a link between the two. By 'good' I mean not only how we judge the conceptual and methodological approach that underpins the research, but how much the study adds to our understanding of how people relate to the media in the process of 'audiencing'. Looking back at the audience research that has had most impact on the ways in which 'we' (and here I mean the academic community of audience researchers) think about people and their media practices, it is clear that these studies are extremely diverse in their approach and their methodologies. However, they appear to have one thing in common: that is, at their best, they vividly illuminate a set of audience practices at a particular time and in a particular context that 'makes sense' at the same time as they change or expand the ways in which we might think about the audience experience.

A modest proposal

Given the ongoing ferment in the field of audience research, a ferment that is probably not going to go away anytime soon, I'd like to conclude with some questions and some suggestions on how audience research might be conducted in the future based on the lessons of the past. The first involves a reconsideration of the relationship between the researcher and the researched. What if we considered both the researcher and the researched as being involved in the co-construction of meaning about the experience of audiencing that may lead to the 'self-realization' implicit in Adrian Athique's (2016) discussion of the sociological imagination? To take this even further, I'd like to suggest that media audience research might involve a reciprocal element in which both the researcher and researched may adopt the position of student and teacher.

For example, in undertaking research into the role of television in migrant women's lives, I am aware that they are teaching me about the dimensions of their experience at the same time as I may be acting as a facilitator in a process of self-realization, as they explore just how and why television did or didn't matter to them during their period of acculturation to Australia. Inviting people to tell the 'story' of their experience as an audience therefore invites them to participate in the reflexive project of self-realization. As Anthony Giddens has pointed out, the reflexive project of the self consists in 'the sustaining of coherent, yet continuously revised, biographical narratives' (Giddens, 1991,

p. 5). In other words, it's the stories we tell about ourselves that help us make sense of who we are and that lead me to advocate for a kind of media audience research that is of value to both the researcher and the researched in the co-creation of meaning and social understanding. Inevitably, I would argue, this research involves a (re)turn to and a reconsideration of ethnographic methods as the most useful in a research project that seeks to understand audiencing in the practice of everyday life.

Ethnography, however, has had something of a bad rap over the years ever since Virginia Nightingale's critique of what was identified as the 'ethnographic turn' in cultural studies during the 1980s and early 1990s (Nightingale, 1989). As was then pointed out, research that was being characterized as ethnographic at that time bore little relationship to ethnography as it might be conducted within anthropology. More recently, reflecting on the future of media audience research in 2006, while David Morley acknowledged that 'ethnography is a fine thing', he was also concerned about the dangers of 'anecdotalism' (Morley, 2006, p. 106). We should not, he argues, 'mistake the vividness of the examples it offers us for their general applicability'; he goes on to suggest that the process of extrapolation from ethnographic examples is one that needs to be handled with particular care (Morley, 2006, pp. 106–107). According to Morley, what is required instead is both a 'horizontal' or micro analysis of the various ways in which people consume the media well as a 'vertical' or macro dimension that addresses the social structures that may obtain and the transmission of ideology and power. Together, he describes these as a 'bifocal mode of vision', noting that neither perspective reveals the whole truth (Morley, 2006, p. 112).

While Morley may be sceptical of an ethnographic approach that never rises above the level of the anecdotal, British anthropologist Daniel Miller is quite clear that the 'ultimate ambition' of anthropology involves a kind of extremism: that is, the desire to balance the parochial (or what Morley might call the horizontal or micro), with a desire to theorize about humanity as a whole (the vertical and the macro) on a wildly ambitious scale (Miller, 2011, p. 2005). This 'bifocal mode of vision' is clearly evident in Miller's study of Facebook users in Trinidad, a Caribbean island where he has been undertaking fieldwork for over 20 years. While this study begins with 12 vivid portraits of different people from different walks of life in Trinidad and their engagement with Facebook (the parochial), the final three chapters offer an analytical interpretation of what these portraits suggest about how

Facebook might function in Trinidad and more generally in the world (the macro). Ultimately it is Miller's deep immersion in the culture of everyday life in Trinidad that enables him to come to a set of understandings about the particular role that this specific media platform has played in this culture, and to speculate on what Facebook might actually 'be' for these people and others.

Miller subsequently offers 15 theses about what Facebook might mean for personal and community relationships before considering the other kinds of transformations it has effected on people's experience of both time and space. While Miller acknowledges that such processes are ongoing and will inevitably continue to change, what this study affords is a compelling account of a specific set of media practices at a particular moment in time that illuminates not only the activities of a particular audience segment but also how a platform such as Facebook might be adopted and adapted for very different purposes. For example, Miller argues that Facebook in Trinidad is better known as *Fas*book or *Maco*book. While to be *fas* in the Trinidadian idiom is to try and get to know a person rather too quickly, to be *maco* is to be too nosy, constantly prying into other people's business (Miller, 2011, p. 159). Given that Facebook as a platform enables both of these cultural traits to be enacted with ease, Miller argues that there is a 'natural affinity between the propensity within the infrastructure of Facebook itself and the cultural inclination of the Trinidadians' (p. 159). Indeed, when Facebook appeared in Trinidad, it seemed to the Trinidadians as if someone in the USA had invented an 'instrument' that was the 'purest expression of Trinidadian culture' (Miller, 2011, p. 160).

Jay Hasbrouck is another anthropologist who considers that 'ethnographic thinking' can be of value in a broad range of applied settings, including within business and industry. As Hasbrouck notes, when compared to traditional forms of applied research, such as surveys and focus groups, ethnography can provide a much deeper understanding of a culture from the perspective of those within it: an understanding that may be invaluable in the provision of services and systems as well as new products (Hasbrouck, 2018, p. xv). While 'big data' may offer detailed information on consumer behaviour, what, when and where it happens, it can't always tell us why. Ethnographic thinking, on the other hand, 'provides an interpretive lens – one that offers new ways to see how cultural worlds are organized and offer frameworks for thinking about how they are formed and how they evolve and interact' (Hasbrouck, 2018, p. 2).

Rather than being driven by a prescribed set of procedures, ethnography, Hasbrouck suggests, may well involve 'strategic wandering' (Hasbrouck, 2018, p. 18). This entails exploring a particular field of interest in a deliberately random way, given that this randomness may lead to the kinds of surprise that a good researcher should always be prepared to encounter. According to Hasbrouck, ethnography thus necessarily involves the expanding of awareness, the deferring of judgment and the need to adapt thoughtfully to circumstances that may well arise during the course of the research, even as the researcher immerses themselves more fully into the process in order to understand the context better. Inevitably, this understanding will involve not only interpretation but also holistic thinking; that is, stepping outside the frame in order to see the big picture, since without this combination of interpretation and analysis (the micro and the macro), Hasbrouck warns, ethnographic practices risk becoming simply a matter of cultural translation. The goal of the researcher is to then communicate the findings in a storied form that is of relevance to those for whom it is intended and which invites readers to imagine a 'whole other world' while empathising with the experience it reveals (Hasbrouck, 2018, p. 89). It is in the writing of such stories, Hasbrouck argues, that ethnographers develop their interpretations and form the insights that are grounded in the cultural phenomenon of everyday lived experiences (Hasbrouck, 2018, p. 89). What is interesting about this latter point is that it identifies writing as an essential part of the ethnographic method.

As an illustration of ethnography in practice, Hasbrouck tells the story of his encounter with Anit in Cairo in the spring of 2006 in the course of a project focusing on the use of technology in the home among the emergent middle class in four different countries (Hasbrouck, 2018, pp. 16–17). Anit, aged 24, lived with her parents and three younger sisters in a large apartment on the third floor of an apartment building. After tea, Anit offered to show Hasbrouck and his research assistant some pictures she had taken of her young niece on her laptop which was charging in her bedroom. As this sharing of images was proceeding, Hasbrouck noticed some of the other technologies in the room that Anit had not included in her inventory of the everyday technologies that she regularly used. These included two mobile phones, a landline phone, a small TV and a dusty laptop hidden under an assortment of stuffed animals and notebooks.

When asked about this PC, Anit explained that this was her old PC from when she was in school, that it was 'broken' and had too many viruses. Although this incident didn't appear to be important, as Hasbrouck notes over the course of the whole project they discovered a similar pattern in other encounters. Thus, rather than discovering how new technologies were being *integrated* into the daily lives of the emerging middle classes in these localities, what they discovered was that there was a great deal of *disintegration* too, and that the 'neglect' of technologies like desktop PCs was widespread. Ultimately these insights enabled the company for whom Hasbrouck was conducting the research to develop a 'healthy-PC' initiative that focused on automating software updates and virus resolutions while also, it might be observed, cutting down on technological waste.

The value of an ethnographic approach to research media practices is also well illustrated by Sarah Pink, Heather Horst, John Postill, Larissa Hjorth, Tania Lewis and Jo Tacchi in their book entitled *Digital Ethnography* (2016). Here they outline a proposal for how ethnography might be used to explore the digital 'as part of the world we co-inhabit with the people who participate in our research', suggesting that in conducting digital ethnography the researcher is most likely to be 'in mediated contact with participants rather than in direct presence' (Pink et al., 2016, p. 3). For Pink and her co-authors, ethnography is thus perceived as a way of practising research involving a 'family of methods' that belongs to no one discipline in particular but that might be of value to many (Pink et al., 2016, p. 3).

In outlining this approach to digital ethnography, Pink et al. propose five key principles that may also be of value in thinking about a different kind of approach to media audience research (2016, pp. 8–13). *Multiplicity*, it is argued, involves adopting a *unique* approach to each research question rather than assuming that one approach or methodological tool is suitable for all; *Non-digital-centricness* implies *decentring* the media as the focus of the research in order to acknowledge how a specific media practice is inseparable from other aspects of experience; *Openness* entails being open to collaborations with other disciplines; while *Reflexivity* requires going beyond the simple notion of 'bias' to acknowledge the *subjectivity* of the research encounter and the explicatory nature of any form of ethnographic writing. Lastly, they advocate for an *Unorthodox* approach to the dissemination of findings, including the use of project blogs, websites and visual forms of communication. In the ensuing chapters in their book, these principles are put into practice with regard to the exploration of digital media experiences and practices in relation to specific events, localities and social worlds.

When it comes to the multiplicity of approaches that are modelled in the studies that follow, the sheer diversity of the various methods that are embraced under the umbrella of ethnography is impressive. These methods include asking people to recount a day in their life as well as inviting them to re-enact specific activities or practices; they may also be asked to keep diaries, using screen shots and images to recount their activities. Other innovations include extending the concept of observation to include the digital technologies that are now available: this would include inviting people to use GoPro wearable cameras to record 'a day in the life' of their everyday media encounters or to conduct a video tour of the spaces in which they live. Clearly, while this approach and these methods may be well suited to the task of revealing the role of the digital media in the practice of everyday life, the most pressing question here is, how might this relate to media audience research?

Media audiencing – In conclusion?

The argument presented here is that media audiencing takes place on a continuum of experience, attention and practice that extends not only over a day but over a lifetime. In order to understand one aspect of this activity, there is a need to be aware of the whole. Similarly, media audiencing as a practice is related to all the other dimensions of a person's lived experience, and there is a need to take account of these too. There are therefore two dimensions to undertaking research in media audiencing. While the first relates to the range of media experiences a person may have had, the other relates to their life experience more generally, their social and cultural context.

When people are asked to reflect on their media audiencing, they are usually being invited to focus on, and account for, their engagement in a specific media practice at a specific moment in time. Such an account might be enabled by a range of different research methods as discussed, including 'a day-in-the-life' video that might well be used as a conversation starter to focus in on the other dimensions of a person's experience that enables the media practice in question to come into focus. However, this process of accounting for media audiencing requires both the researcher and the researched to engage in a form of reflexive practice in order to co-produce a story that will illuminate both the micro and the macro dimensions of the audience experience while enabling (hopefully) a degree of self-realization. In this way questions of meaning making, of identity construction, and an understanding of the social and cultural dimensions of the audience experience, may be brought into focus. While such an approach inevitably begins with the individual, an audience research project might well include a range of such accounts that will enable the researcher to draw out a range of broader themes or propositions relating to the media practice in question.

We then come to the question of dissemination. Who is the audience for this research? How should it be framed? How best to tell a story about this research in a compelling and accessible way using different forms of dissemination? While media audience research may well be interested in the viewpoint of the researched, for the most part it has been a one-sided endeavour – even when the research method used is ethnography. The researcher conducts the research, writes it up and it is published in the form of an academic article or a book that may not be accessible to those about whom it is written. While this may be inevitable in some cases, there may well be a need, and an occasion, for different kinds of 'research reports'. Indeed, the digital environment in which we are now located enables a wide range of modes of publication and sharing, including through blogs and dedicated websites.

One of the most interesting explorations in media audience research that I have been involved in lately has involved inviting undergraduate students to undertake autoethnographic research that they have shared on the WordPress sites that they are required to create as a part of their studies. This has also involved a requirement that they read and comment on each other's experiences to open up a productive dialogue about aspects of their very different and sometimes shared experiences. While this has occurred in an academic context, I can see no reason why it might not also be used as a model for conducting audience research involving participants who are also motivated and willing to share their experiences in a safe and moderated environment.

While this mode of undertaking media audience research may be an unrealistic ideal, it nevertheless points to some of the key questions that we need to consider when we undertake a media audience research project. They include the following, although these are far from exhaustive:

- What are the motives underpinning this research?
- How is the 'audience' to be located/assembled/constructed?

- What is the position of the researchers in the landscape of enquiry and what do they bring to this study?
- How do the media practices of audiencing that are being explored relate to the practices of everyday life?
- How should we conceptualize these?
- What methods of enquiry are most appropriate to this study?
- How best should it be described?
- Who is the audience for this research?

And last but by no means least:

- What is the value of this research for the researchers and the researched?

So – rather than concluding with a set of answers, I am concluding with a set of questions and the proposition that the future of media audience research, like the future of the media, is yet to be written. However, if we are to gain any insight into the evolving practice of audiencing, what we need now, as in the past, are vivid accounts of the ways in which the media is imbricated in people's daily lives in order to understand how and why this experience matters to them or not. What we also need to reflect on is the value of these accounts not just to society at large but also to those who participate. When it comes to audience research, we're all in this together.

Reference List

Adorno, Theodor W. and Max Horkheimer. 1944. *Dialectic of enlightenment*. Trans. J. Cumming. London and New York: Verso.

Albury, Kathy, Paul Byron and Ben Matthew. 2013. *Young people and sexting in Australia: ethics, representation and the law*. University of New South Wales and ARC Centre of Excellence for Creative Industries, Queensland University of Technology.

Althusser, Louis. 1971. *Lenin and philosophy and other essays*. New York and London: Monthly Review Press.

Ang, Ien. 1985. *Watching Dallas: soap opera and the melodramatic imagination*. London and New York: Methuen.

Ang, Ien. 1991. *Desperately seeking the audience*. London and New York: Routledge.

Athique, Adrian. 2016. *Transnational audiences*. Cambridge: Polity Press.

Attorney General's Department. 2010. Literature review on the impact of playing violent video games on aggression. *Attorney-General's Department*, September, Canberra, Australia. https://www.classification.gov.au/about-us/research-and-publications/literature-review-impact-playing-violent-video-games-aggression.

Austen, Jane. 1987. *Northanger Abbey*. New York: Barnes & Noble Classics.

Bacon-Smith, Camille. 1992. *Enterprising women: television fandom and the creation of popular myth*. Philadelphia: University of Pennsylvania Press.

Balnaves, Mark and Tom O'Regan. 2012. *Rating the audience: the business of media*. Gordonsville: Bloomsbury.

Barker, Martin (ed). 1984. *The video nasties: freedom and censorship in the media*. London: Pluto Press.

Barker, Martin. 2006. 'I have seen the future and it is not here yet ...' or, on being ambitious for audience research. *The Communication Review*, 9(2). 132–141.

Barker, Martin. 2018. The rise of the Qualiquants: on methodological advances and ontological issues in audience research. *Participations: Journal of Audience and Reception Studies*, 15(1). 439–452.

Barker, Martin. 2019. Editorial introduction. *Participations: Journal of Audience & Reception Studies*, 16(1). 1–2.

Barker, Martin and Ernest Mathijs (eds). 2008. *Watching Lord of the Rings: Tolkien's world audiences*. New York: Peter Lang.

Barker, Martin and Julian Petley (eds). 1998. *Ill effects: the media/violence debate*, 2nd edn. Oxford: Routledge.

Barthes, Roland. 1967. The death of the author. In *Aspen: The Magazine in a Box 5 +6*. http://www.ubu.com/aspen/aspen5and6/threeEssays.html#barthes. Accessed 21 August 2019.

Bausinger, Hermann. 1984. Media, technology and daily life. *Media Culture & Society*, 6(4). 343–351.

Baym, Nancy. 2015. *Personal connections in the digital age*, 2nd edn. Cambridge: Polity.

Beaumont, Peter and Amanda Holpuch. 2018. How the *Handmaid's Tale* dressed protests across the world. *The Guardian*, 3 August. https://www.theguardian.com/world/2018/aug/03/how-the-handmaids-tale-dressed-protests-across-the-world.

Bird, Elizabeth. 2003. *The audience in everyday life: living in a media world*. New York and London: Routledge.

Blitt, Barry. 2016. 1 February cover art. *The New York Times*. https://www.newyorker.com/culture/culture-desk/cover-story-2016-02-01. Accessed 27 August 2019.

Blumer, Herbert. 1933. *The movies and conduct*. New York: The Macmillan Company.

Blumler, Jay G. and Elihu Katz. 1974. *The use of mass communication*. Beverly Hills: Sage.

Bourdieu, Pierre. 1984. *A social critique of the judgement of taste*. London: Routledge & Kegan Paul.

Bowles, Kate. 2011. 16 mm cinema as rural community fundraiser in the 1950s. In *Exploration in new cinema history: approaches and case studies*, ed. R. Maltby, D. Biltereyst and P. Meers, 310–321. West Sussex: Wiley-Blackwell.

boyd danah. 2014. *It's complicated: the social lives of networked teens*. New Haven: Yale University Press.

Boyle, Amy. 2020 forthcoming. 'They should have never given us uniforms if they didn't want us to be an army': *The Handmaid's Tale* as transmedia feminism. *Signs* 45 (4).

Brennen, Bonnie S. 2017. *Qualitative research methods for media studies*, 2nd edn. New York: Routledge.

Brown, Mary. E. 1994. *Soap opera and women's talk: the pleasure of resistance*. Thousand Oaks: Sage.

Bruns, Axel. 2008. *Blogs, Wikipedia, Second Life and beyond: from production to produsage*. New York: Peter Lang.

Buckingham, David. 2003. *Media education: literacy, learning and contemporary culture*. Cambridge: Polity Press.

Burgess, Jean and Josh Green. 2018. *YouTube: online video and participatory culture*, 2nd edn. Cambridge: Polity Press.

Butsch, Richard. 2000. *The making of American audiences: from stage to television, 1750–1990*. Melbourne: Cambridge University Press.

Cavicchi, Daniel. 2014. Fandom before 'fan': shaping the history of enthusiastic audiences. In *Reception: texts, readers, audiences, history*, vol. 6, 52–72. University Park: Penn State University Press.

Couldry, Nick. 2004. Theorising media as practice. *Social Semiotics*, 14(2). 115–132.
Couldry, Nick. 2012. *Media, society, world: social theory and digital media practice*. Cambridge: Polity.
Couldry, Nick. 2014. The necessary future of the audience…and how to research it. In *The handbook of media audiences*, ed. V. Nightingale, 213–229. Malden: Wiley Blackwell.
Cunningham, Stuart and David Craig. 2017. Being 'really real' on YouTube: authenticity, community and brand culture in social media entertainment. *Media International Australia*, 164. 71–81.
Dafoe, Allan. 2015. On technological determinism: a typology scope conditions, and a mechanism. *Science, Technology, & Human Values*, 40(6). 1047–1076.
de Certeau, Michel. 1984. *The practice of everyday life*. Trans. S. Rendall. Berkeley: University of California Press.
Dubois, Elizabeth and Grant Blank. 2017. The echo chamber is overstated: the moderating effect of political interest and diverse media. *Information, Communication and Society*, 21(5). 729–745.
Edgar, Patricia and Hilary McPhee. 1974. *Media she*. Melbourne: Heinemann.
Finn, Kavita V. M. 2017. *Fan phenomena: Games of Thrones*. Bristol: Intellect Books.
Fiske, John. 1989a. *Reading the popular*. Winchester: Unwin Hyman.
Fiske, John. 1989b. *Understanding popular culture*. Winchester: Unwin Hyman.
Fiske, John. 1992. Audiencing: a cultural studies approach to watching television. *Poetics*, 21(4). 345–359.
Frazer, Elizabeth. 1987. Teenage girls reading *Jackie*. *Media, Culture and Society*, 9(4). 407–425.
Giddens, Anthony.1991. *Modernity and self-identity: self and society in the late modern age*. Cambridge: Polity Press.
Gillespie, Marie. 1995. *Television, ethnicity and cultural change*. London: Routledge.
Goffman, Erving. 1976. *Gender advertisements*. London and Basingstoke: The Macmillan Press.
Gray, Ann. 1994. Behind closed doors: video recorders in the home. In *Boxed in: women and television*, ed. H. Baehr and G. Dyer, 38–54. London: Pandora Press.
Gray, Jonathan. 2003. New audiences, new textualities: anti-fans and non-fans. *International Journal of Cultural Studies*, 6(1). 64–81.
Gray, Jonathan, Cornel Sandvos and C. Lee Harrington. 2017. *Fandom: identities and communities in a mediated world*, 2nd edn. New York: New York University Press.
Gray, Jonathan, Jean Burgess, Paul Frosh, Anthony Fung, Myria Georgious and Lori Kido Lopez. 2019. Editorial. *International Journal of Cultural Studies*, 22(1). 3–8.
Greenfield, Adam. 2017. *Radical technologies: the designs of everyday life*. London: Verso Books.

Greenslade, Roy. 2016. Here's the truth: 'fake news' is not social media's fault. *The Guardian*, 23 November. https://www.theguardian.com/media/greenslade/2016/nov/23/heres-the-truth-fake-news-is-not-social-medias-fault.
Gregg, Melissa. 2011. *Work's intimacy*. Cambridge: Polity Press.
Gregg, Melissa. 2018. *Counterproductive: time management in the knowledge economy*. Durham, NC and London: Duke University Press.
Grossberg, Lawrence. 1988. Wandering audiences, nomadic critics. *Critical Studies*, 2(3). 377–391.
Hall, Stuart. 1973. Encoding/decoding in the television discourse. *Paper for the council of Europe colloquy on 'training in the critical reading of television language'*, 1–19. Council & the Centre for Mass Communication Research, University of Leicester, September.
Hall, Stuart. 1980. Encoding/decoding. In *Culture, media, language: working papers in cultural studies, 1972–1979*, ed. S. Hall, D. Hobson, A. Lowe and P. Willis, 117–127. London: Routledge.
Hall, Start. 1986. Introduction. In *Family television: cultural power and domestic leisure*, ed. D. Morley, v–vii. London: Comedia.
Hall, Stuart and Tony Jefferson. 1975. Resistance through rituals: youth subcultures in post-war Britain. In *Working papers in cultural studies*, ed. S. Hall and T. Jefferson, 7/8. Birmingham: Centre for Cultural Studies.
Harré, Rom. 1979. *Social being: a theory for social psychology*. Maryland: Rowman & Littlefield.
Harré, Rom. 1984. *Personal being: a theory for individual psychology*. Cambridge, MA: Harvard University Press.
Harvey, Adam. 2014. *Game of Thrones* piracy war: choice says Foxtel has itself to blame for illegal downloading of hit show. *ABC News*, 18 June. https://www.abc.net.au/news/2014-06-17/choice-backs-australians-who-pirate-game-of-thrones/5530710?pfmredir=sm.
Hasbrouck, Jay. 2018. *Ethnographic thinking: from method to mindset*. New York and London: Routledge.
Heiselberg, Lene. 2018. Expanding the toolbox: researching reception of TV program with a combination of EDA measurements and self-reports in applied audience research. *Participations: Journal of Audience & Reception Studies*, 15(2). 18–36.
Hermes, Joke. 1995. *Reading women's magazines: an analysis of everyday media use*. Cambridge: Polity Press.
Herzog, Herta. 1941. On borrowed experience. *Studies in Philosophy and Social Science*, 11. 65–95
Herzog, Herta. 1944. What do we really know about daytime serial listeners? In *Radio research 1942–1943*, ed. P. F. Lazarsfeld and F. N. Stanton, 3–34. New York: Essential Books.
Herzog, Herta. [1941] 2004. On borrowed experience: an analysis of listening to daytime sketches. In *Mass communication and American social thought: key texts, 1919–1968*, 139–154. Lanham: Rowman & Littlefield.

Hill, Annette. 2005. *Reality TV: audiences and popular factual television*. London and New York: Routledge.
Hill, Annette. 2018. *Media experiences: engaging with drama and reality television*. London: Routledge.
Himmelweit, Hilde T., Abraham N. Oppenheim and Pamela Vince. 1958. *Television and the child: an empirical study of the effect of television on the young*. London: Oxford University Press.
Hoggart, Richard. 1976. Foreword. In *Gender advertisements*, vii–viii. London and Basingstoke: The Macmillan Press.
Horace Hugh, Walpole. 2001. *The castle of Otranto*. Oxford: Oxford University Press.
Huyssen, Andreas. 1986. *After the great divide: modernism, mass culture, postmodernism (theories of representation and difference)*. Bloomington and Indianapolis: Indiana University Press.
Idato, Michael. 2019a. After a bloody decade, and almost a billion dollars winter is finally here. *Sydney Morning Herald*, 15 April. https://www.smh.com.au/entertainment/tv-and-radio/after-a-bloody-decade-and-almost-a-billion-dollars-winter-is-here-20190414-p51e1r.html..
Idato, Michael. 2019b. Winter arrives at long last. *Sydney Morning Herald*, 15 April.
Isbister, Katherine. 2016. Why Pokemon Go became an instant phenomenon. *The Conversation*, 16 July. https://theconversation.com/why-pokemon-go-became-an-instant-phenomenon-62412.
Ito, Mitzuko, Daisuke Okbe and Misa Matsuda (eds). 2006. *Personal, portable, pedestrian: mobile phones in Japanese life*. Cambridge, MA and London: MIT Press.
Jenkins, Henry. 1992. *Textual poachers: television fans and participatory culture*. New York: Routledge.
Jowett, Garth S., Ian C. Jarvie and Kathryn H. Fuller. 1996. *Children and the movies: media influence and the Payne Fund controversy*. Cambridge: Cambridge University Press.
Katz, Elihu and Ruth Katz. 2016. Revisiting the origin of the administrative versus critical research debate. *Journal of Information Policy*, 6(1). 4–12.
Keller, Jessalynn and Jessica Ringrose. 2015. But then feminism goes out the window!'. Exploring teenage girls' critical response to celebrity feminism. *Celebrity Studies*, 6(1). 132–135.
Kolowich, Lindsay. 2016. How the news feed algorithms work on Facebook, Twitter and Instagram. *HubSpot*, 14 April; updated 30 April 2019. https://blog.hubspot.com/marketing/how-algorithm-works-facebook-twitter-instagram.
Lange, Patricia. 2014. *Kids on YouTube: technical identities and digital literacies*. New York: Routledge.
Leavis, Frank and Denys Thompson. 1933. *Culture and environment: the training of critical awareness*. London: Chatto & Windus.
Liebes, Tamar. 2003. Herzog's 'On borrowed experience': its place in the debate over the active audience. In *Caronic texts in media research*, ed. Elihu Katz,

John Durham Peters, Tamar Liebes and Avril Orloff, 39–52. Cambridge: Polity Press.

Liebes, Tamar and Elihu Katz. 1993. *The export of meaning: cross cultural readings of Dallas*. Cambridge: Polity Press.

Livingstone, Sonia. 2002. *Young people and new media: childhood and the changing media environment*. London: Sage.

Livingstone, Sonia. 2009. Half a century of television in the lives of our children. *Annals AAPS*, 625. 151–163.

Livingstone, S., L. Haddon and A. Gorzig (eds). 2012. *Children, risk and safety on the internet: kids online in comparative perspective*. Bristol: The Policy Press.

Livingstone, Sonia, Giovanna Mascheroni and Elisabeth Staksrud. 2018. European research on children's internet use: assessing the past and anticipating the future. *New Media and Society*, 20(3). 1103–1122.

Lobato, Raymond. 2019. *Netflix nations: the geography of digital distribution*. New York: New York University Press.

Lopierdinger, Martin and Bernd Elzer. 2004. Lumière's arrival of the train: cinema's founding myth. *The Moving Image*, 4(1). 89–118.

Lotz, Amanda D. 2003. Communicating third-wave feminism and new social movements: challenges for the next century of feminist endeavor. *Women and Language*, XXVI(1). 1–9.

Lotz, Amanda. 2014. *The television will be revolutionized*, 2nd edn. New York: New York University Press.

Madianou, Mirca. 2014. Beyond the presumption of identity? Ethnicities, cultures and transnational audiences. In *Global handbooks in media and communication research: the handbook of media audience*, ed. V. Nightingale. West Sussex: John Wiley & Sons Ltd.

Maltby, Richard. 2011. New cinema histories. In *Explorations in new cinema history: approaches and case studies*, ed. Richard Maltby, Daniel Biltereyst and Philippe Meers, 3–40. Malden: Wiley-Blackwell.

Maltby, Richard, Daniel Biltereyst and Philippe Meers. 2011. *Exploration in new cinema history: approaches and case studies*. West Sussex: Wiley-Blackwell.

Maslow, Abraham M. 1943. A theory of human motivation. *Psychological Review*, 50(4). 370.

Mathijs, Ernest and Janet Jones. 2004. *Big Brother international: formats, critics and publics*. London: Wallflower Press.

McDuling, John. 2019. How *Game of Thrones* changed television ... and the business of television. *Sydney Morning Herald*, 14 April. https://www.smh.com.au/business/companies/how-game-of-thrones-changed-television-and-the-business-of-television-20190414-p51dyq.html. Accessed 28 August 2019.

McKee, Alan. 2001. *Australian television: a genealogy of great movements*. Sydney: Oxford University Press.

McKee, Alan. 2016. *FUN!: what entertainment tells us about living a good life*. Palgrave Entertainment Industries series. London: Palgrave Pivot.

McKee, Alan, Katherine Albury and Catharine Lumby. 2008. *The porn report*. Melbourne: Melbourne University Press.

McKinnon, Scott. 2016. *Gay men at the movies: cinema, memory and the history of a gay male community*. Bristol: Intellect.

McNair, Brian. 2002. *Striptease culture*. London: Routledge.

McRobbie, Angela. 1982. *Jackie*: an ideology of adolescent femininity. In *Popular culture past and present*, ed. B. Waites, T. Bennet and G. Martin, 263–283. London: Croom Helm.

McRobbie, Angela and Jenny Garber. 1975. Girl and subcultures. In *Resistance through rituals: youth subcultures in post-war Britain*, Working papers in cultural studies, ed. S. Hall and T. Jefferson, 7/8. Birmingham: Centre for Cultural Studies.

McRobbie, Angela and Trisha McCabe. 1981. *Feminism for girls: an adventure story*. Oxford: Routledge.

Michelle, Carolyn, Charles H. Davis, Ann Hardy and Craig Hight. 2017. *Fans, blockbusterisation, and the transformation of cinematic desire: global receptions of the* Hobbit *trilogy*. London: Palgrave Macmillan.

Michelle, Carolyn, Charles David, Ann Hardy and Craig Hight. 2019. 'Response to Martin Barker's 'Rise of the Qualiquants'. *Participations: Journal of Audience and Reception Studies*, 15(2). 376–399.

Miller, Daniel. 2011. *Tales from Facebook*. Cambridge: Polity Press.

Mills, Wright. 2000 [1959]. *The sociological imagination*. Oxford: Oxford University Press.

Mitchell, Amy and Rachel Weisel. 2014. Political polarization and media habits: from Fox News to Facebook, how Liberals and Conservatives keep up with politics. *Pew Research Centre*, October. https://www.pewresearch.org/wp-content/uploads/sites/8/2014/10/Political-Polarization-and-Media-Habits-FINAL-REPORT-11-10-14-2.pdf.

Mittell, Jason and Chuck Tryon. 2016. America's fake news problem predator. *Vox*, 21 November. https://www.vox.com/culture/2016/11/21/13682574/fake-news-facebook-fox-news-conservative-radio.

Modleski, Tania. 1982. *Loving with a vengeance: mass-produced fantasies for women*. London and New York: Methuen.

Moores, Shaun. 2018. *Digital orientations: non-media-centric media studies and non-representational theories of practice*. New York: Peter Lang.

Morley, David. 1986. *Family television: cultural power and domestic leisure*. London: Comedia.

Morley, David. 2006. *Media, modernity and technology: the geography of the new*. London: Routledge.

Morley, David and Charlotte Brunsdon. 1980. *The 'Nationwide' audience: structure and decoding*. London: BFI.

Münsterberg, Hugo. 1916. *The photoplay: a psychological study*. Oxford: Routledge.

Murdock, Graham. 1997. Reservoirs of dogma: an archaeology of popular anxieties. In *Ill effects: the media/violence debate*, ed. M. Barker and J. Petley, 2nd edn, 50–86. Oxford: Routledge.

Napoli, Philip M. 2010 *Audience evolution: new technologies and the transformation of media audiences*. New York: Columbia University Press.

Nielsen. 2015a. Screen wars: the battle for eye space in a TV-everywhere world. *The Nielsen Company (US), LCC*, 4 January. https://www.nielsen.com/us/en/insights/report/2015/screen-wars-the-battle-for-eye-space-in-a-tv-everywhere-world/#. Accessed 23 August 2019.

Nielsen. 2015b. Sixty-nine percent of global consumers think that face-to-face interactions are being replaced by electronic ones. *The Nielsen Company (US), LCCI*, 4 January. https://www.nielsen.com/ug/en/press-releases/2015/sixty-nine-percent-of-global-consumers-think-electronic-interactions-are-replacing-face-to-face-ones/. Accessed 23 August 2019.

Nielsen. 2018. The Nielsen total audience report: Q2 2018. *The Nielsen Company (US), LCC*. https://www.nielsen.com/wp-content/uploads/sites/3/2019/04/q2-2018-total-audience-report.pdf. Accessed 27 August 2019.

Nightingale, Virginia. 1989. What's 'ethnographic' about ethnographic audience research? *Australian Journal of Communication*, 16. 50–63.

Nightingale, Virginia. 2014. *The handbook of media audience studies*. Malden: Wiley-Blackwell.

Ólafsson, Kjartan, Sonia Livingstone and Leslie Haddon. 2014. Children's use of online technologies in Europe: a review of the European evidence base. *EU Kids Online*LSE. London: EU Kids Online. Revised edition.

Pink, Sarah, Heather Horst, John Postill, Larissa Hjorth, Lewis Tania and Jo Tacchi. 2016. *Digital ethnography*. London: Sage.

Press, Andrea L. 2006. Audience research in the post-audience age: an introduction to Barker and Morley. *The Communication Review*, 9(2). 93–100.

Priest, Susanna H. 1996. *Doing media research: an introduction*. Thousand Oaks: Sage.

Radcliffe, Ann. 1974. *The mysteries of Udolpho*. London: Penguin.

Radway, Janice. 1984. *Reading the romance: women, patriarchy and popular literature*. Chapel Hill: University of North Caroline Press.

Radway, Janet. 1988. Reception study: ethnography and the problems of dispersed audiences and nomadic subjects. *Cultural Studies*, 2(3). 359–376.

Ringrose, Jessica, Rosalind Gill, Sonia Livingstone and Laura Harvey. 2012. A qualitative study of children, young people and 'sexting': a report prepared for the NSPCC. National Society for the Prevention of Cruelty to Children, London.

Rorty, Richard. 1998. *Achieving our country: leftist thought in twentieth-century America*. Massey lectures. Cambridge, MA: Harvard University Press.

Ross, Karen. 1997. But where's me in it? Disability, broadcasting and the audience. *Media, Culture and Society*, 4(19). 669–677.

Ross, Karen and Virginia Nightingale. 2003. *Media and audiences: new perspectives*. Maidenhead: Open University Press.

Ruddock, Andy. 2001. *Understanding audiences: theory and method*. London: Sage.

Ruddock, Andy. 2013. *Youth and media*. London: Sage.

Rush, Emma and Andrea La Nauze. 2006. *Corporate paedophilia: sexualisation of children in Australia*. Deakin: Australia Institute.

Schramm, Wilbur, Jack Lyle and Edwin B. Parker. 1961. *Television in the lives of our children*. Stanford: Stanford University Press.
Sless, David. 1986. *In search of semiotics*. London and Sydney: Croom Helm.
Strauss, Anselm L. 1987. *Qualitative analysis for social scientists*. Cambridge: University of Cambridge.
Sullivan, Rebecca and Alan McKee. 2015. *Pornography: structures, agency and performance*. Cambridge: Polity Press.
Trier-Bieniek, Adrienne (ed.). 2015. *Feminist theory and pop culture: a text reader*. Rotterdam: Sense Publishers.
Turkle, Sherry. 2011. *Alone together: why we expect more from technology and less from each other*. New York: Basic Books.
Turnbull, Sue. 1993. Accounting for taste: the moral and aesthetic dimension of media practices. *Melbourne Studies in Education. Special issue: feminism and education*, 95–106.
Turnbull, Sue. 1997. On looking in the wrong places: Port Arthur and the media violence debate. *Australian Quarterly*, 69(1). 41-49.
Turnbull, Sue. 1998a. Once more with feeling: talking about the media violence debate in Australia. In *Ill effects: the media/violence debate*, ed. M. Barker and J. Petley, 2nd edn, 111–125. Oxford: Routledge.
Turnbull, Sue. 1998b. Dealing with feeling: why girl number twenty still doesn't answer. In *Teaching popular culture: beyond radical pedagogy*, ed. D. Buckingham, 88–106. London: UCL Press.
Turnbull, Sue. 1998c. Dear Anne Summers: microfeminist responses to the media. In *Wired-up: young people and the Electronic media*, ed. S. Howard, 153–169. London: UCL Press.
Turnbull, Sue. 2008a. Understanding disappointment: the Australian book lovers and adaptation. In *Watching Lord of the Rings: Tolkien's world audiences*, ed. M. Barker and E. Mathjis, 103–110. New York: Peter Lang.
Turnbull, Sue. 2008b. Beyond words: the return of the king and the pleasures of the text. In *Watching Lord of the Rings: Tolkien's world audiences*, ed. M. Barker and E. Mathjis, 181–190. New York: Peter Lang.
Turnbull, Sue. 2017. Top dogs and other freaks: *Wentworth* and the re-imaging of *Prisoner Cell Block H*. In *Television antiheroines: women behaving badly in crime and prison drama*, ed. M. Buonanno, 181–198. Bristol: Intellect.
Turnbull, Sue and Marion McCutcheon. 2019. Quality vs value: the case of the *Kettering Incident*. In *A companion to Australian cinema*, ed. Felicity Collins, Jane Landman and Susan Bye, 391–415. West Sussex: John Wiley & Sons, Inc.
Tyron, Chuck. 2013. *On-demand culture: digital delivery and the future of movies*. New Brunswick: Rutgers University Press.
van Zoonen, Liesbet. 1994. *Feminist media studies*. London: Sage.
Webster, James G. 2014. *The marketplace of attention: how audiences take shape in a digital age*. Cambridge, MA: MIT Press.
Wertham, Frederic. 1954. *Seduction of the innocent*. New York: Rinehart & Company.

Williams, Linda. 1999. *Hard core: power, pleasure and the 'Frenzy of the Visible'*. Berkeley: University of California Press.
Williamson, Judith. 1978. *Decoding advertising: ideology and meaning*. London: Marion Boyers.
Willis, Paul. 1977. *Learning to labour: how working-class kids get working class jobs*. New York: Columbia University Press.
Winn, Marie. 1977. *The plug-in drug: television, children and the family*. New York: Viking Press.
Winn, Marie. 2002. *The plug-in drug: television, computers and family life*. New York: Penguin Group.
Winship, Janice. 1987. *Inside women's magazine*. London: Pandora.
Wollaston, Sam. 2017. The *Handmaid's Tale* review: the best thing you'll watch all year. *The Guardian*, 29 May. https://www.theguardian.com/tv-and-radio/2017/may/29/handmaids-tale-review-best-thing-youll-watch-all-year.
YouTube. 2018. Top trending videos of 2018. *YouTube*, 6 December. https://www.youtube.com/playlist?list=PLSTz8jpJdr5rPetsXm_wr55L467SQ-T-D. Accessed 27 August 2019.

Index

active audience   2, 18–19, 32, 35–6, 42, 52, 103
advertising/advertisements   5, 10, 30, 32, 70, 78, 89
Ailes, Roger   70
Albury, Katherine   76–80
Althusser, Louis   6, 66, 99
Ang, Ien   4, 19, 31, 86–9
The Apprentice   71
Athique, Adrian   84, 114, 120
attention economy   33
audience, definitions of   13, 20, 21, 30–31, 107, 110, 122
audiencing   13, 19, 20, 27–30, 37, 39–60, 96, 110, 112, 119–20, 125, 127
Austen, Jane   43

Bacon-Smith, Camille   61
Barker, Martin   17, 19, 99, 109, 111, 113, 118, 119
Barthes, Roland   65–66
Bausinger, Hermann   6–7, 8, 16, 57, 60
Baym, Nancy   40, 92
Beaumont, Peter   106
Beyoncé   102–3
Big Brother   28, 32–3
Bird, Elisabeth   27
Blumer, Herbert   45, 115
The Book of Kells   40–41
Bourdieu, Pierre   46, 88, 89, 104
Boyd, danah   92, 96–7, 114
Boyle, Amy   105–6
Brexit   68, 69
British Broadcasting Corporation (BBC)   48

Brown, Mary E.   43, 100–101
Brunsdon, Charlotte   67
Buckingham, David   3, 34, 114
Butsch, Richard   86

Cambridge Analytica   66, 67
The Castle of Otranto   42
causality   34–5, 46, 62
Cavicchi, David   104
celebrities   10–11, 81–2, 102–3
Child's Play   3, 35
cinema   12, 21, 22, 24, 34, 46–49, 51, 86, 107
  studies   2, 3
Collins, Joan   11, 12
Corporate Paedophilia   78
The Cosby Show   12
Couldry, Nick   27, 118
Cressey, Paul G.   46–48, 49, 51, 52, 92, 115
cultural studies   3, 5, 6, 28, 109, 121

Dafoe, Allan   39–40, 53
Dallas   4, 86–8, 89, 101
David, Charles H.   111, 117–9
de Certeau, Michel   10, 101
Digital Ethnography   124
disability   107–108
dystopian   34, 106

Edgar, Patricia   5
Elzer, Bernd   44
encoding and decoding   66–7
ethnicity and race   10, 66, 71, 73, 79, 86, 89–1, 113
ethnography   4, 46, 90, 97, 121–26

139

family 6, 8, 9, 10–13, 23, 28, 50, 51, 53–4, 56–58, 90–1
fans/fandom 18, 25, 36, 61, 88, 101–105, 110
femininity 11, 102
feminism/feminist 4–5, 43, 75, 99, 102–3
   activism 5
   critique 4–5, 100, 102
Fiske, John 28, 42, 101–104
Fox News 69–70
Frazer, Elizabeth 99–100
Fujimoto, Kenichi 98

Game of Thrones 30, 36, 62, 63, 111
Garber, Jenny 5, 6
gay culture 107
gender 26, 53–4, 66, 91, 98–103
   representations of 4–5, 12, 102–3, 106
   roles 8, 13, 54, 59
Gender Advertisements 5
generational divides 11–12, 32, 79, 84, 90–91, 97
genre 4, 42–3, 54
   documentary 43, 70, 83
   gothic 42–43
   gothic romance 4
   horror 35
   romance 43, 100
   satire 43, 70
   soap opera 4, 11, 43, 54, 86, 88, 90, 100–101
   teen film 8
Gillespie, Marie 89–91, 92
Goffman, Erving 5
Gray, Ann 54
Gray, Jonathan 88, 93, 104–6, 109
Greenfield, Adam 21
Greenslade, Roy 69
Gregg, Melissa 58–9
Guardian 69
Gutenberg, Jonas 41

Hall, Stuart 5, 66–7, 72
The Handmaids Tale 106

Hardy, Ann 111, 117–19
Harré, Romano 7
Harrington, Lee C. 104–6, 109
Hasbrouck, Jay 122–4
Hauser, Philip 45
Heiselberg, Lene 74
Herzog, Herta 100–101
Hight, Craig 111, 117–19
Himmelweit, Hilde 50–51, 52, 55, 56
The Hobbit 111, 117–19
Holpuch, Amanda 106
Hugo 43
Huyssen, Andreas 43

ideology 5, 6, 61, 66–9, 72, 81, 88, 99–100, 111, 117, 121
Implicit Tensions 75
Ito, Mizuko 98

Jackie 99–100
Japan 25, 89, 98
Jefferson, Tony 5
Jenkins, Henry 36, 42, 101, 104

Katz, Elihu 17, 86, 89, 113
Katz, Ruth 113
Keller, Jessalynn 102–3
Kolowich, Lindsay 69–70

Lange, Patricia 83–4, 96
Learning to Labour 6
Leavis, Frank 3, 48
legacy media 2, 21, 24
Liebes, Tamar 86, 89, 100–101
The Lion King 35
Livingstone, Sonia 34, 51, 54–6, 94, 96, 114
Loiperdinger, Martin 44
Lord of the Rings 111, 119
Lotz, Amanda 4, 5, 32
Lumby, Catharine 76–80
Lyle, Jack 52

Madonna 11, 12, 102
magazines 25, 39, 43, 71, 78, 91, 99
Maltby, Richard 48–49

Mapplethorpe, Robert 75
Married at First Sight 29
Marxism 6, 39, 113, 114
masculinity 6, 10, 56, 98
Maslow, Abraham 29
McKee, Alan 4, 29, 42, 75–7, 114
McKinnon, Scott 107
McNair, Brian 77
McPhee, Hilary 5
McRobbie, Angela 5, 43, 99
Media, Culture & Society 6
media affect vs. effect 34–5, 62–3, 74
media practices 7, 16–18, 57, 85, 112–15, 120, 122–7
Media She 5
media technologies 2, 21, 24–6, 29–32, 34, 37, 39–60, 75, 77–80, 92–3, 113, 123–5
Michelle, Carolyn 111, 117–19
Miller, Daniel 121–2
Mills, C. Wright 114
Mittell, Jason 70
mobile devices 21, 23–5, 31, 55, 58, 79, 92, 94, 95, 98, 109
Modleski, Tania 4, 43, 61, 100–102
Moores, Shaun 7, 112
moral career 7, 8, 12
Morley, David 53–4, 55, 67–8, 72, 109, 121
Münsterberg, Hugo 44
Murdoch, Rupert 70
Murdock, Graham 98
The Mysteries of Udolpho 42

Napoli, Philip 25, 30–31
Nationwide 67–8
Neighbours 4, 90–91
Netflix 60, 111–12
New Yorker 71–2
Nielsen company, the 31–3, 39
Nightingale, Virginia 17–18, 90, 121
non-media-centric 7, 27, 112, 124
Northanger Abbey 43

Omnicore 81
Outfoxed 70

Parker, Edwin B. 52
Payne Fund Studies 34, 44–50, 73, 93, 115
performance of self 9–11
The Photoplay: A Psychological Study 44
Plato 93
The Plug in Drug: Television, Children and the Family 53
podcasts 39
Pokémon Go 26
popular culture 3, 5, 43, 100, 101, 105
popular media 3, 4, 5, 8, 10, 11, 13, 14, 15, 48
pornography 42, 75–78, 85
Port Arthur Massacre 35
post-war 1, 5, 49, 56
Prisoner: Cell Block H 4
propaganda 68, 72
Punjabi 89–91

Q methodology, the 117–20

Radcliffe, Ann 42
radio 2, 21, 28, 39, 55, 60
Ramsey, Mason 82
reality TV 28, 32
Richards, Lyn & Tom 9
Ringrose, Jessica 77–9, 93, 102–3
Rorty, Richard 71
Ross, Karen 17–18, 107–8
Rudd, Kevin 76

Sanders Peirce, Charles 64
Sandvoss, Cornel 104–5
Schramm, Wilbur 50, 52–3, 96
Scorsese, Martin 43
screen violence 4, 20, 42, 51, 63, 74–5
semiotics 5, 64–6, 71, 99
sex 46, 47, 61, 73, 75, 77, 104

sexism 79
sexting 61, 77–80
sexuality 4, 11, 47, 66, 71, 75–80, 102
sexual violence 79, 106
The Simpsons 70
Sless, David 116
social class 1, 2, 6
social media
　Facebook 26, 30, 62, 68–70, 78, 79, 121–2
　Twitter 26, 85
social psychology 18, 39, 93, 115
Star Trek 36, 61

The Taxi-Dance Hall 46
technological determinism 39, 53, 56
television and family life 11–13, 21, 23, 50–58, 90
Textual Poachers 36, 61, 101
Thompson, Denys 3, 48

Trier-Bieniek, Adrienne 102
Trinidad 121–2
Trump, Donald 68–72, 85, 106
Tryon, Chuck 70, 111

uses and gratifications 17–18

van Zoonen, Liesbet 4, 99
violent video games 73, 74
Viva 87
vlogs 62, 80–81, 83

Walpole, Hugh 42
Webster, James G. 19, 85
Williams, Linda 42, 75
Williamson, Judith 5
Willis, Paul 6
Winn, Marie 53
working-class 1, 6, 34, 59, 61, 86, 98

YouTube 25, 26, 56–7, 60, 62, 80–84, 96, 110

Printed by Printforce, the Netherlands